The
Exodus

by
Jonathan Burgess

THE STORY THAT **HAD** TO BE TOLD

The Exodus
The story that had to be told

ISBN 978-1-905989-37-9

 **CAUSEWAY PRESS (N.I.)**

Causeway Press
9 Ebrington terrace
Londonderry
BT47 6JS

Cover picture. Lorcan Doherty Photography

Contents

Inntroduction

The Play

The Transcripts

We acknowledge the assistance from the following:

THE EXODUS by Jonathan Burgess

The term of the exodus has always been one that has conjured instant memories for me, although these were not my own, as my parents' decision to leave Abercorn Road was taken when I was less than a month old when my father witnessed the shooting of a soldier not far from our front door. The memories I have are from people, exclusively family members, mentioning, (barely more than that) their experience of departing the Cityside as I grew up in the Waterside. Despite the sheer volume of Protestants that left, it was never something that was discussed in any formal or even informal way within the community, but everyone had their story. There can be few people, if any, from the Protestant community, native to the city in the late 1960's / early 1970's that do not have a family story of their movement away, whether to the Waterside or further afield.

It is this absence of a voice that prompted me to embark on this project – aspiring towards it for over ten years and actively working on it for four.

In my opinion the exodus would rival the Siege in terms of significance towards the Protestant community within the city and has become as momentous to the Protestant heritage in the city as those events of 1689. It has, though, never been marked or given appropriate consideration. This project has aimed, if only in a small way, to address this. As a very slow research process developed, as information about this project permeated into the community, more and more people have come forward to speak – not with the easy and well-rounded speech of an often recounted tale, but with an insecure recollection with some unsure of what I wanted.

Just their story.

Those who have spoken to me will see an aspect of themselves in this production, some will even hear the words they spoke to me given back to them as lines in the mouths of Trevor and Emma. To attempt to represent this whole aspect of a community's heritage through the life of one household will always be an incomplete one, but nothing less than hearing every story would facilitate this. This production is a starting block that will hopefully inspire people to tell their story, either for inclusion on the website or book which will be produced as part of this project.... or to other people from within and without the Protestant community.

I remember reading in one of the papers that there would be a greater number of people from the Chinese community on the west bank of the Foyle, than from the Protestant community in 1997. In a city and country not known for the significance of its ethnic diversity, this was quite a stark indicator of the profile of the Protestant community within Londonderry.

With the award of the UK City of Culture and the genuine movement towards a shared future, this is an aspect of the heritage of this city which should be acknowledged if that aspiration towards a shared future is going to be realised in any real way.

I would like to thank the funders, Heritage Lottery, Derry City Council and Community Relations Council for their support and the actors and production staff that have brought this show to life. My sincerest thanks though, must also go to the ordinary people who have told me their stories and guided this project to fruition.

Jonathan Burgess
Londonderry - April 2011

Blue Eagle Productions is an independent theatre and production company formed in 2002 and is based in Londonderry, Northern Ireland. The company produces main-stage touring productions, theatre-in-education shows, living history projects and festivals. The company also undertakes bespoke commissions from both the private and voluntary sectors. Recent credits include "The Blue Eagle George Farquhar Theatre Festival", "Fair Faa Ye", "Fair Faa Ye, USA" and "Noose Or Necklace".

Jonathan Burgess is a freelance theatre producer, director and writer. Aside from running Blue Eagle Productions, he is the director of the annual pantomime at The Millennium Forum and Millennium Forum Youth Theatre. He has produced for Sole Purpose Productions, Echo Echo Dance Theatre Company and The Playhouse. Recent writing credits include "The Pride", for The Pride Of The Orange And Blue Flute Band; "Far Off Fields" and "The Parting" for The Alley Theatre / Balor Theatre; "Muckbeth" for The Patrician Hall, Carrickmore; "Fair Faa Ye", "Fair Faa Ye, USA" and "Noose Or Necklace" for Blue Eagle Productions and "The Siege Story" for The Maiden City Festival.

The Exodus

By
Jonathan Burgess

"The Exodus" was first performed at The Waterside Theatre, Londonderry
on Wednesday 13th April 2011.

The Cast for this production were (in order of appearance)

Emma Hamilton – Sorcha Shanahan
Trevor Hamilton – James Lecky
Radio Announcer – Stephen Bradley
Alec Lyttle – Arthur Oliver-Brown

Set & Costume Designer – Helen Quigley
Lighting Designer – Andrew Orr
Sound Designer – Paul Rooney
Stage Manager – Arthur Oliver-Brown

The production was written and directed by Jonathan Burgess and
produced by Blue Eagle Productions.

THE EXODUS by Jonathan Burgess

Act 1

Lights up to reveal a sitting room at the turn of the 1970's in Londonderry. On the stage left wall is a window looking out to the street, in front of which sits a small two-seater sofa. Downstage of the window is a flip-top music centre. In the upstage left corner is a door, which leads out to the hallway and the front door. Upstage centre is a dining room table and four chairs, behind which to the right is a standard lamp. Against the back wall is a low press, which has the 'good' crockery in it. Above it on the wall are three pictures – an Honourable Discharge Certificate from World War 1, a passing out picture from the RUC and a picture of men standing under an Orange Arch in the desert. In the stage right corner is another door which leads out to the kitchen. On the stage right wall is a fireplace, which has a mirror directly over it. A chair with a footstool is set beside it. A radio sits on a small table on the upstage side of the fireplace, along with a couple of folded newspapers. The furniture in the room is past its best, but the room is clean and tidy. As the scene is established the radio is playing pop music of the day, followed by a radio jingle before another tune starts. While the first song has been fading out, a woman (Emma) in her mid-twenties enters the room hastily with a plate of dinner, comprising of a chop, potatoes and carrots, which she sets down at the table that has been set for one, on the stage right side of it, looking hurriedly back at the clock on the mantle-piece as she does so. She is dressed in a frock, with a house coat over the top. She looks around to make sure all is in place as the second song comes on. As it starts to play, she moves and sits down in the chair next to the radio, an air of melancholy comes across her. As the first line of the song ends, the front door opens and "Hello" is heard from off. She hurriedly turns off the radio and stands as the door from the hall opens and a man (Trevor) in his late-forties enters. He is dressed in a black three piece suit and is carrying another suit jacket. He has his coat over his arm. He sets the coat over the back of the chair closest to the door and the suit jacket on the sofa.

Emma: Hello, Daddy.

Trevor: Hello, love. How are you?

Emma: Grand. Grand. There's your tea. (*realising she has forgot something*) Oh!

Emma disappears to the kitchen, as Trevor takes off his jacket, hanging it over the back of the chair before sitting down. Emma reappears a few moments later with the teapot. She pours tea into his teacup. She sets the teapot on the hearth and then sits down beside him in one of the upstage centre chairs. Trevor starts to saw at the chop without much success.

Trevor: Are you not having any?

Emma: I've had mine already.

Trevor: Oh. (*pause*) Well, would you not have a cup of tea at least?

Emma gets up from the table and exits to the kitchen. Trevor, meanwhile, has managed to dislodge a part of the chop which he pops in his mouth and starts to chew.... and chew. Emma has come back in from the kitchen and moves to the table where she pours a little milk into her cup and then moves to the hearth where she pours herself a cup of tea. She stands with her back to the fire and watches her father intently as he continues to chew.

Emma: (*tentatively*) How is it?

Trevor: (*taking a mouthful of tea to swallow over the chop*) Lovely.

Emma: (*suspicious*) Really?

Trevor: (*kindly*) Maybe just a wee bit dry.

Emma: Gravy. I forgot the gravy. (*she moves quickly into the kitchen, where saucepans can be heard rattling*)

Trevor: Emma, love. (standing) Emma! I don't need it. It's
             grand as it is.

*The rattling stops and Trevor waits for Emma to reappear in the
kitchen doorway. She is holding a saucepan.*

Emma: It's no bother, Daddy. I can make you some gravy.
             I didn't empty out the pan.

Trevor: No. Honestly, it's fine. It is. Now, come on and
             finish your tea.

Emma: Are you sure?

Trevor: Yes. I'm sure.

Emma rejoins him at the table.

Trevor: *(after swallowing over another well chewed piece
             of the chop)* Your mother was the exact opposite.
             She would have had the plate swimming in gravy.
             Her dinners were more like soup than dinner.

Emma: But you never said anything to her.

Trevor: *(pause)* No.

*They both fall into silence for a moment. Trevor dislodges another
piece of the chop and pops it into his mouth and starts the chewing
process all over again.*

Trevor: Is the Girls Brigade on tonight?

Emma: *(reluctantly)* Aye. *(pause)* But I was thinking of
             just missing it tonight.

Trevor: Come on, now. You can't be doing that.

Emma: *(pause)* I don't know if I'm ready to.....

Trevor: Emma, you can't sit in the house every night.

Emma: But I don't know if I want to go back. Not just yet.

Trevor: *(gently)* It's been six weeks.

Emma gets up from her seat and moves to stand in front of the hearth, with her back to Trevor.

Trevor: Sure, you've been back at your work for over a month.

Emma: Aye, daddy, but I **have** to go to my work.

Trevor: *(insistent)* And you have to go back to GB. You have a responsibility to those wee girls. *(pause)* It's the enrolment service in church this Sunday and you can't miss that.

Emma's head drops. She pauses for a moment, collects herself and then turns.

Emma: It just seems so soon.

Trevor: *(hesitantly, with difficulty)* We have to get back to a normal way of going.

Emma: *(shocked and reproachful)* How can you say that?

Trevor: Because we have no choice. *(pause)* Do you think your mammy would have wanted us sitting around letting the dust settle on us? It's hard. I know it is, but we have to get on with it.

Emma: But everything is so different.

Trevor: I know, love, but we can't lie down and pretend the world isn't turning outside that door anymore. *(pause)* I have to get into that bed on my own every night. And wake up in it every morning and remember all over again that she's not there.

Emma: I'm sorry, daddy. I didn't mean to.... I didn't think.

Trevor: It's alright. But we have to push on.

Emma: *(pause)* Alright, daddy. *(pause, then reluctantly)* I'll go up tonight.

Trevor: Good girl.

Emma: But what are you going to do? I don't like the thought of leaving you on your own.

Trevor: I'll be fine. *(indicating the jacket on the sofa opposite him)* I have that suit-jacket to finish stitching. The fella that ordered it is coming for it in the morning.

Emma: It's not like you to be behind.

Trevor: *(resuming the end of his dinner) (off-handed)* Aw, we had to get out this afternoon. There was a bomb-scare outside the police station and we were out for two hours, so it'll have to be done tonight. I would have stayed down at the shop, but there was no way of getting in touch with you to let you know not to cook the tea and I knew once I got back up here this evening I wouldn't want to go out again.

Emma: *(indicating the plate)* I bet you wish now that you'd taken the effort to get in touch.

Trevor: Don't be silly. And, anyway, there's no guarantee that something else wouldn't happen down that town. And sure, we won't have that problem of not being able to get in touch after Friday. *(pause, smiling)*

Emma: *(lost)* What?

Trevor: The new telephone.

Emma: Oh aye, the new telephone.

Trevor: Now, go on away with you and get changed.

Emma nods and moves to start clearing away the tea dishes.

Trevor: Leave those, I'll get them. Go on, or you'll be late.

Emma exits. Trevor takes one last mouthful of his dinner and starts to tidy up, exiting to the kitchen with his dinner plate, Emma's cup, the milk jug and the salt and pepper shakers. He comes back in and lifts his own cup onto the mantelpiece, stooping to turn on the radio. He is startled by the radio jingle from the pop music channel and retunes the radio to a news channel. He then moves to lift the jacket and set it on the table before getting out his sewing box from the low press along the back wall.

Voice Over: *Further unrest continued today in east Belfast following the weekend's confrontation between republicans and loyalists in the Short Strand area of the city. Police and army were able to restore calm after violence flared in the area again around lunchtime when a number of buses were hijacked and set on fire, but tensions remain high. Bus services to east Belfast and Hollywood and Newtownards have been cancelled and police are advising that anyone travelling in that area of the city stay away from the lower Newtownards Road at Bryson Street where several hijacked vehicles are still burning. And now for the weather. Low lying fog in the early part of tomorrow will clear around mid-morning, but sporadic showers will continue throughout the day in the west of the Province before moving east in the later part of the afternoon.*

During the bulletin Emma enters dressed in her Girls Brigade (GB) officer's uniform.

Emma: Right daddy, I'm going to head up here.

Trevor: Good girl.

Emma: I'll be down after nine.

Trevor: I'm sure I'll be wred up by that stage.

Emma moves over and gives him a kiss on the cheek and then turns and exits. Trevor watches her go, waiting to hear the front door close before he turns back to his work.

Voice Over: *This is a police message for all key-holders in the Strand Road area of Londonderry between Waterloo Place and Clarendon Street to return to their premises as a suspect device has been reported as being left in the area. That's a police message for all key-holders in the Strand Road area of Londonderry between Waterloo Place and Clarendon Street to return to their premises as a suspect device has been reported as being left in the area.*

During the repetition of the announcement, Trevor sets down his scissors in disgust and sighs deeply before moving to the radio and turning if off, pulling on his coat, checking for his keys, then turning off the standard lamp and moving towards the door where he switches off the main light before exiting into the hall where he turns out the hall light and exits.

Black out.

Voice Over: *(overlapping) This is a police message for key-holders in the Carlisle Road area of Londonderry to return to their premises as a suspect device is reported as having been left in the area.*

This is a police message for key-holders in the Church
Street area of Coleraine to return to their premises as a
suspect device is reported as having been left in the area.
This is a police message for key-holders in the Castle
Street area of Armagh to return to their premises as a
suspect device is reported as having been left in the area.
This is a police message for key-holders in the
Darling Street area of Enniskillen to return to their
premises as a suspect device is reported as having
been left in the area.
This is a police message for key-holders in the Campsie
Avenue area of Omagh to return to their premises as a
suspect device is reported as having been left in the area.
This is a police message for key-holders in Donegal
Square North to return to their premises as a suspect
device is reported as having been left in the area.
This is a police message for key-holders in the
Duke Street area of Londonderry to return to their
premises as a suspect device is reported as having
been left in the area.

Lights up to reveal Emma sitting on the edge of the sofa, she has her
shoes off, but is still dressed in her GB uniform and has a mug of tea
on the floor beside her. She is reading the paper avidly, in shock. She
shakes her head as she turns the pages, but continuously glances at
the clock on the mantelpiece. She takes some folded sheets of paper
out of her handbag and peruses them (they advertise new houses in
Newbuildings, several miles outside the city). After several moments,
she hears a sound at the door and stuffs the pieces of paper into the
newspaper. She sits up and waits expectantly sitting looking at the
door. A few moments pass and nobody enters. She gets up and goes
out into the hall. She enters a few moments later with an envelope,
which she looks at. She turns it over, but there is no writing on it.
She opens the envelope and takes out a card - it is a mass card. Again

there is no writing on it. She is puzzled and goes to look out the window tentatively. As the curtains fall back into place, she hears the key turn in the front door and puts the card in her pocket and reaches into the newspaper, pulling the loose sheets she had out of it and hurriedly opening the top of the record player, throwing them inside. The door to the living room opens and Trevor enters. He is carrying several loose items of clothing, suit jackets, trousers etc. He is exhausted as he lurches towards the table and drops the bundle on to it. He is panting and out of breath.

Emma: *(standing up and moving to him)* Daddy, are you alright?

Trevor: Aye, love. Aye. *(pausing to catch his breath before continuing)* It's....

Emma: *(examining the clothes)* What's all this?

Trevor: Work from the shop.

Emma: *(not understanding)* What?

Trevor: *(still catching his breath)* Work.

Emma: *(still not understanding)* You went all the way back down to the shop to get work? *(agitated)* What are you doing going out at night? *(recovering)* What time are you planning to sit up to tonight?

Trevor: After you left, there was a police message on the radio and I had to go back to the shop.

Emma: *(reacting)* What was it?

Trevor: They thought there had been another one of those blooming incendiary devices left in one of the shops on the Strand and they asked the key-holders to go down and have a look.

Emma: And they put a call out over the radio for you just to toddle off down there into that!

Trevor: *(continuing)* But anyway they were getting the place cordoned off and everybody out of the area, so I just grabbed what was on the cutting table, because I don't know if they'll have that cleared by the morning and I'm not getting behind. I'm not losing a day's work over the head of them boys, so I'll work from here tomorrow. I put a sign up on the side door to say that anybody that wants to can still come up here and collect their clothes from the house on time. Business as usual.

Emma: Well it's hardly that! And what about that wee skitter that works with you? Sure you know he won't come round here. It's more than he can do to even be civil to you in the shop.

Trevor: Well, he can come or not if he wants to, but I have work to do and customers to see to. Mr. Campbell doesn't pay me to be sitting idle. So them that wants their clothes can come here and them that wants to work can come here also. *(pause, considering)* To be fair now, he hasn't been so bad since your mammy died. He's eased off a wee bit, especially seeing what we had to go through the day of the funeral. I think he's a wee bit embarrassed.

Emma: And so he should be! I still don't see him coming round here to sit and do work at this table. *(pause, calming)* When I think of what we had to go through.

Trevor: Don't talk about it.

Emma: Don't talk about it? Daddy, my mammy has been dead six weeks and I still haven't seen the grave.

Trevor: *(snapping)* What did you want me to do? Take on the IRA? *(then recovering)* I'm sorry, love. Sorry. I could just have been doing without that run out tonight.

Emma: *(conciliatory)* I don't want you to take on anybody. *(anger rising again)* I just want to visit my mammy's grave and put flowers on it. And I can't because they have it all blocked off. *(holding out the newspaper)* And will I ever see it, or will they have it blocked off forever?

Trevor: Can we just leave it? Please?

Emma: *(rising again)* I don't want to leave it. And from what is going on in the town, I don't think them boys are going to leave it either.

Trevor: What has got into you tonight?

Emma: Have you seen this paper? Have you seen the amount of people moving out and all because of them boys and what they're doing. Up round Bishop Street. Sure the people in the Fountain have barricaded themselves in! *(picking up the paper)* Have you seen this? It's happening everyday, more and more leaving.

Trevor: Emma, you shouldn't be letting that affect you.

Emma: How can I not, daddy? It makes me so angry.

Trevor: *(snapping again)* You're angry? It wasn't you that had to go cap in hand to the IRA to ask them if you could bury your wife. *(pause as he recovers)* So, we'll just leave it?

A long pause in which Trevor drops his gaze and goes back to his tailoring. Emma watches him for a moment, stunned into no reaction.

Emma: *(pause)* And David couldn't go to the cemetery either.

Trevor: *(affirming grimly)* And David couldn't go to the cemetery either. *(giving her a look which tells her that the conversation is over)*.

Emma: *(meekly, after a pause to let the subject pass)* Do you want supper, daddy?

Trevor: *(after a moment)* I'll just take a cup of tea, if there is one?

Emma: I'll get it for you.

Emma exits to the kitchen as Trevor starts to spread out the various clothes and sort them into two piles of trousers and jackets. There is the odd waistcoat.

Emma: *(from off, her tone still agitated)* That was twice last week and now this week where you've had to go out.

Trevor: *(absentmindedly focusing on his work)* It's terrible.

Emma: *(from off)* Why can't the police or the army search the premises?

Trevor: I suppose if we do it, then we'll be more likely to know if something is out of place.

Emma: *(entering with a cup of tea and biscuit on the saucer)* I don't like it. It's very dangerous. Why doesn't Mr. Campbell come in and do it? It's his shop after all.

Trevor: I'm the manager, I suppose. And I'm the closest. Sure he's away out beyond Drumahoe.

Emma: I still don't like it.

Trevor: So you said. *(pause, stopping to set down the scissors and look at her)* Look Emma, one day soon all this is going to stop.

Emma: I don't know about that.

Trevor: You're old enough to remember the town before all this started. There are too many good people in this town to let it go on. I'm sure there's plenty working hard to get this stopped. And they will. The ministers and the priests are preaching against this type of behaviour from the pulpits every Sunday.

Emma: Then why isn't it getting through? The people who are doing this to the country aren't influenced by anybody, because if they were it would have stopped long ago. It started out as weeks and months, but that's turned into years and all you hear on that radio day-in day-out is shootings and bombings all over the Province. How long are we going to have to live with this?

Trevor: I'm sure it won't be much longer before people come round. They'll see the error of their ways and the government will get it back under control. These boyos can't last. They don't have any support in the communities.

Emma: And how many more people are going to die before it does end? Another five hundred? A thousand, maybe.

Trevor: Nothing like that. *(seeing that Emma is shaking with fear)*

Emma: Look daddy..... *(she starts to breakdown)*

Trevor: *(softening and concerned, he moves to her)*
Emma. Emma? What's wrong?

Emma: *(reaching for the words)* I'm just frightened,
daddy, I'm sorry. *(pause)*

Trevor: Come on now, Emma.

Emma: I'm sorry daddy. I'm so sorry, but you see even
the thought of those police messages that call you
out at night. They scare me so much. *(pause)*
I've been in the town and heard gunfire and not
known where it was coming from. I've been in shops
and seen the windows shake in their frames when
a bomb went off, but daddy, there is nothing that
frightens me more than the sound of that man's
voice on the radio when that police message comes
through. I hate it. I always wish it's somewhere else,
and then I feel guilty because that means that some
other family is sitting wondering if their daddy is
going out and might not come back again. Every
time you go out all I do is listen for the click of the
lock on the door, so I can start to breathe again.
I'd rather it was me going out to check the shop.

Trevor: *(trying to smile it off)* Uck, now Emma....

Emma: *(turning on him)* You don't know. You don't
know what it's like. Lying in a quiet house waiting
for one sound. *(pause)* Or the other.

Trevor: *(realising how upset she is)* I had no idea.

Emma: How could you? You're never the one sitting here
doing the listening. Frightened to breathe too hard
in case you missed the sound of the key in the lock.

I remember one night you must have come in
when I was out at the toilet. I must have laid
awake for ages listening for the key in the lock.
And then I heard you snoring. *(long pause, in
which Trevor rises and moves thoughtfully to
the mantelpiece)* Mammy was exactly the same.

Trevor: What?

Emma: Just before Christmas it came through on the radio
and you had to go out. *(pause as she looks at him
to see if he remembers)*

Trevor: *(quietly)* I don't remember.

Emma: It was the day before David came down. Mammy
was due in the hospital the next day and he was
going to meet us up there.

Trevor: I remember that.

Emma: But not going out the night before?

Trevor shakes his head.

Emma: I remember going in to make sure mammy was
asleep and when I opened the door I saw her sitting
on the edge of the bed, looking out the window.
She must have got up and opened the curtains. Can
you imagine the effort that must have taken out of
her seeing how sick she was? I don't think she even
heard me coming into the room, she was just staring
out the window into the night. The room was
freezing too. I had to call out to her twice before
she heard me. "Your daddy isn't home yet is he?"
was what she turned to me and said, but she wasn't

asking me a question. Of course I got her back into bed and wrapped up again, but she didn't say anything to me while I was doing it. She was still listening. We both were. I told her I would nip in and tell her as soon as you got back. Then she said to me, "It would be wild if something happened to your daddy tonight and David coming down tomorrow". That was all she said. *(turning to Trevor)* I stood on the landing in the dark for over two hours waiting for you to come back that night. When I heard the key turn in the lock I nipped in to tell her you were home. I saw her face where the light from the landing fell across the bed. Her eyes were wide open and the tears were running down her cheeks. She'd heard you come in. I could see the tension had left her face. I couldn't even speak. I just closed the door and went off to hide in my bed.

Trevor: I never knew.

Emma: How would you, daddy?

Trevor: *(pause as he moves to sit)* I'm sorry.

Emma: *(moving quickly to him and kneeling beside his chair)* It's not your fault, daddy. How could it be your fault? But it might be you that faces the consequences.

Trevor: Look Emma, I know this town. I'll be fine. We'll be fine. The good people will win through in the end. All this stuff about what colour your coat is, is going to fade away and be like it was before, when it didn't matter.

Emma: *(petulantly)* The only thing that seems to matter at the moment is what colour your coat is.

Trevor: *(rising and moving to the table and back to his*

work) There's no talking to you tonight.

Emma: *(after considering for a moment she also rises and moves to him at the table)* Daddy, did you hear about what happened in Bishop Street last night? Fourteen Protestant families moved out of Gordon Place in one night. Fourteen! They had to send a coal lorry to get all their furniture out. And there was no police or army there to protect them. They had to send for people from the Fountain to help them. Fourteen families moved, daddy! Fourteen homes ruined!

Trevor: Why are you so angry?

Emma: Why are you not? *(pause, then exasperated)* I just want to go and visit my mammy.

Trevor: Right, well if that's what it is we'll go up to the cemetery on Sunday.

Emma: I don't want to go. I wouldn't feel safe walking up there.

Trevor: But that's what I'm saying, you can't let that put you off, this is still your town.

Emma: It doesn't feel like it. And if that's how you feel, why haven't you been up since the funeral? *(pause, Trevor has nothing to say)* I'm going on to bed. *(quietly)* Good night, daddy.

Trevor: Good night.

Emma: *(pause, as she stops in the doorway)* I just want to go and see my mammy.

Trevor moves towards the doorway as if to go after Emma. When he reaches the door he stops - his head dropping. He hears a sound of people running past the window and goes to check. When he sees no one there, he moves to the record player. On opening the lid, he discovers the paper about Newbuildings, which Emma had thrown in there earlier. He pauses for a moment reading it, his expression darkening. He recovers himself and turns on the record player, which starts to play the hymn "How Great Thou Art". He then moves back towards his seat by the fire, lifting the newspaper. He sits and starts to read. Loosening his tie, he leans back, his eyes closing. He falls asleep as the lights fade to black.

Lights up to reveal Trevor asleep in the chair with the newspaper across his knee. The hall door opens and Emma enters. She is in a dressing gown. She moves to open the curtains and notices the top of the record player open. The sound of the needle still rotating on the end of the LP can be heard. She bends and lifts the needle off the record, replacing it on its stand. She throws back the curtains and turns to move towards the kitchen. Only then does she notice her father in the chair. She is startled and pauses momentarily to watch him. She moves to him, taking the open newspaper off his knee, she looks at the page he was reading, shaking her head and then closing it. She bends to turn on the radio beside his chair, adjusting the volume to keep it low, before exiting to the kitchen. A news jingle can be heard.

Voice over: A British soldier has been killed overnight in a bomb attack in south Armagh. The soldier, who has not been named, was killed immediately when a booby-trap device exploded in a car on the outskirts of Crossmaglen. The area has been sealed off as it is feared that a secondary device may be in the area. Rioting continued last night in areas of west Belfast and Londonderry. Police and army came under attack whilst army bomb experts in the Strand Road area of the city examined a suspicious device in the area. The section of the Strand Road from Sackville Street to Clarendon Street remains closed. In sport, Derry

City beat Distillery last night 2-1 at The Brandywell, with a penalty in injury-time after trailing one-nil with ten minutes to go in the match. And finally the weather. The day will start brightly in the west, with clear skies, but these will become overcast in the afternoon, leading to rain in the early part of the evening. Central and easterly parts of the province will remain dry throughout the day, with rain expected overnight with a chance of frost on high-ground and exposed areas.

Trevor has started to wake up and as the sports report commences he is awake. The sound of a pan being dropped in the kitchen is heard.

Emma: *(entering with teapot and tea cup, pouring tea into cup at the table before moving to the hearth and setting the teapot down on it)* Sorry, daddy. Did I wake you?

Trevor: *(still coming round)* Eh?

Emma: Did I...?

Trevor: *(rising and moving to the table)* No. No... *(flannelling)* I was.... I mean..... No.

Emma: *(exiting to the kitchen she returns with the toast)* Did you sleep down here last night, daddy?

Trevor: What? *(turning off the radio)* No.... I came down early to get on with this suit. My eyes were going together last night. I could barely get the needle threaded. I more or less just followed you up. I came down early, but I must have just dozed off again.

Emma: *(disbelieving)* Oh.

Trevor: *(indicating the suit)* I suppose I better get on with this.

Emma: You're nearly done.

Trevor: Aye, just this last wee bit of lining and that's it. But sure I've plenty to be getting on with.

Emma: I heard on the news that the Strand's still closed.

Trevor: Aye, I thought that it might be. That's why I brought those other clothes up with me. The policeman at the bottom of Clarendon Street told me last night that there would be no way they would have it open before the army boys got a look at it in the daylight. *(indicating the jacket he has been working at)* But sure five minutes will get this one sorted out.

Emma: Here, I'm running late.

Emma exits the room.

Trevor finishes the sewing and sets the finished jacket over the back of the sofa.

Trevor: *(lifting the plate with the toast on it)* Two slices.

Emma comes back in hurriedly, she is dressed in her working frock and has her coat on. She checks herself in the mirror over the fireplace.

Trevor: *(indicating the toast)* Are you taking a slice of that?

Emma: *(absently)* Hmm?

Trevor: Of that toast. You know I don't take two rounds.

Emma: *(looking round)* Sorry, daddy. Force of habit. Why don't you keep the second round and have that with your tea at eleven.

Trevor: It'll be lovely by that stage.

Emma: *(Emma lifts half of the second slice and pops it into her mouth)* Right then. I'll split it with you. *(heading for the door)* I'll be back up at lunchtime.

Trevor: I'll be grand.

Emma: I wasn't thinking about you – I have to eat as well, you know. Half a slice of toast won't keep me going all day.

Trevor: Then take the full slice.

Emma moves back to give Trevor a kiss on the cheek. He smiles as he watches her go, watching the door until he hears it close, then returns to his work. After a moment there is a knock at the door.

Trevor: *(to himself)* Not a moment too soon.

He exits towards the front door. We hear it open.

Alec: *(from off)* Morning chief.

Trevor: *(off, quizzically)* Can I help you?

Alec: *(off)* Phone.

Trevor: *(off)* Eh? Oh right, right. Telephone. You'd better come in.

Alec: *(entering)* I'd have trouble installing it from out there. Right, where do you want it? In the hall, that's where most people have them.

Trevor: *(unsure)* Is that where most people have them? I suppose then.

Alec: It doesn't have to go there.

Trevor: Well, where can it go?

Alec: Anywhere you want chief. I can run it the whole

way up to your bedroom. You could lie in your bed
and take all your calls from there, if you want.

Trevor: I don't know if I'd like that. It might go off in the
middle of the night and scare the life out of me.

Alec: I was only joking.

Trevor: Oh, right. Well, you see I thought if it was in here,
in the heat. There's not a wild lot of room in the hall.
And it could sit on the press there. Could you do that?

Alec: No problem, chief.

*Alec starts to unpack the phone setting it on top of the table, he sets
his tool bag down on the sofa, on top of some of Trevor's clothes.
Trevor moves to lift the tool bag, setting it on the dining chair
beside Alec towards stage right. He starts to fold the clothes from
underneath it, occasionally brushing dirt from items with the back
of his hand, dirt which has come from the tool bag.*

Trevor: Watch the clothes.

Alec: Sorry there, chief.

*Alec starts to work, boring at the skirting board on the on-stage side
of the door. Trevor watches intently over his shoulder.*

Trevor: You won't make too much of a mess, will you?

Alec: Ah, you'll not even know I was here when I'm finished.

Trevor: Is there anything I can do?

Alec: Not really. It's a one-man job. *(pause)* Thirsty work,
all the same.

Trevor: Cup of tea?

Alec: You read my mind, chief.

Trevor: *(sarcastically)* Did I, indeed?

Trevor exits to the kitchen. Alec continues his work. He looks up, searching for his tool bag, which he spots. He gets up and moves to it, swapping the boring tool for a small hammer. He is distracted by a picture on the back wall of David in his RUC passing-out photograph. He starts to look more closely at the pictures, one of which is an Honourable Discharge from the army.

Alec: *(calling off)* I see there have been a few from this house doing their bit.

Trevor enters from the kitchen with two cups of tea and sets them on the table. He is somewhat unnerved by this comment.

Alec: Aw don't worry. I'm doing my bit too.

Trevor: *(slowly)* What do you mean by that?

Alec: UDR. Part-time of course.

Trevor: *(relieved)* Oh. That's my son, David. He's only been in the police for about six months. Well, six months since he came out of training. *(indicating the Honourable Discharge)* And that, that's the wife's father. First World War. I think that one has been on that spot on the wall since he came back. He was at Ypres. Didn't talk about it much. In fact, that certificate would be the only way you would have known he was in the trenches.

Alec: *(indicating a black and white photograph of several men in desert uniform under an Orange arch)* And what's this one here?

Trevor: The handsome one, third from the right is me. 12th of July 1942. North Africa.

Alec: *(impressed)* You built an arch?

Trevor: Well, they weren't letting us back for the parade.

Alec: *(Trevor smiles warmly at the photograph)* Did you think I'd rumbled you there?

Trevor: No. Well, you know.....

Alec: I know. Not something you mention casually in company. There's not many of our crowd left over here.

Trevor: What d'you mean by that?

Alec: A lot of Prods've moved out of here.

Trevor: *(pause, giving him a consideration)* You're not from 'derry, sure you're not?

Alec: Londonderry? *(pause as they both regard each other)* No, I'm not. Belfast.

Trevor: And what brought you here?

Alec: I needed the work.

Trevor: Aye, there's a few can say that. Here. Here's your tea.

Alec: Spot on, chief.

Trevor: *(indicating a cardboard box)* Is that it? The telephone?

Alec: Aye.

Trevor: Can I see it?

Alec: Work away.

Trevor takes the telephone out of the box and examines it. Alec gulps down his tea and goes back to work at the skirting board. Trevor stands up and sets the telephone on the table. He practices lifting it a couple of times, holding it to his ear and mouthing silently into it. He then practices dialling. Alec sits up and watches him, smiling. Trevor lifts the telephone pretending to answer it one last time.

Alec: Hello? Is there anybody there with a telephone for I need to get it wired in?

Trevor is caught, embarrassed. He replaces the handset and passes the telephone to Alec.

Alec: *(laughing)* Don't worry about it, chief. I don't need it all, just the wire. You can keep on practicing if you want. Everybody's the same. After a week, you'll wonder why you bothered getting it installed.

Trevor is embarrassed and moves out to the kitchen.

Alec: Now, all I need is the grippers for the wall and you'll be right as rain.

Trevor: *(re-entering from the kitchen, with the teapot in his hand)* Eh?

He starts to search for the small fixtures, which attach the telephone wire to the wall and can't find them in his tool bag. He stands up and searches in his pockets and then the floor and table.

Trevor: What have you lost?

Alec: The wee fixtures that hold the wire to the wall for round the doorframe and skirting.

Trevor: Aw well, you need those.

Alec: Aye I know, or you'll be tripping over that wire every time you come into the room. Here, check you under that table and I'll see if they got kicked under the sofa.

Trevor moves to take all the chairs out from around the table and

Alec goes in behind the sofa. When both are fully ensconced in their positions the front door opens and Emma enters.

Emma: Daddy?

Trevor: *(from under the table)* Hello love?

Emma: *(hurrying to kneel down)* Daddy, are you alright? Did you fall?

Trevor: Naw. I'm down here looking for the grippers.

Emma: The what?

Alec has popped up from behind the sofa. He is watching Emma, from behind, with a smile on his face.

Alec: Did ye get them?

Emma starts at the voice from behind her and leaps to her feet, where she turns to see Alec smiling at her. She is startled and a little embarrassed.

Trevor: *(making his way out from under the table)* No sign.

Alec: I'll go out and check the van.

Alec exits.

Emma: Who's that?

Trevor: That's the fella who's come to put the phone in.

Emma: He's nice.

Trevor: Eh?

Emma quickly moves to the mirror and starts to fix her hair. She takes her coat off and throws it out into the kitchen.

Trevor: *(realising)* Oh! Here, what are you doing home anyway?

Emma: Bomb-scare on the bridge, so the bottom of

Abercorn Road, Carlisle Road and John Street are all closed. I met Sally and Jean coming back from the town when I got to the top of William Street, so at least I didn't have to go the whole way down. We're going to take a wander down at twelve and see if it's clear at that stage.

Alec comes back in from the van.

Alec: Naw. None there. Look, I'm sorry about that Mr. Hamilton. I'll need to do another run up here to get that sorted out, but I'm away all weekend on patrol and I'm fully booked Monday and Tuesday. D'ye want me to take it out and come back on Wednesday and.....?

Trevor: Naw, just leave it. I'd rather have it up and running. Sure you can come back next week and finish that wee job.

Alec: Right, well I tell you what, I'll come up on Tuesday, after I've got sorted out and do that. It'll only take me two minutes.

Emma: So, you'll be back up on Tuesday?

Alec: Aye.

Trevor: Right, well is that you done?

Alec: I just need to ring through to the exchange now and get them to check the line and that's me?

Emma: Did you get a wee cup of tea?

Trevor: He did.

Emma: I was only being polite, daddy. I'm going to have one and I'll finish off that other half slice of toast.

Alec: *(lifting the receiver and dialling '100')* Hello? This is the engineer. *(pause)* Aye, it's me. Alec. I'm finished putting in this line. The name's Mr. Hamilton and the address is..... *(flicking through)*. That's right. Would you do a ring back, just to check the line? Five, nine, seven, one.

Alec hangs up the telephone. All three of them wait, watching the telephone. A few seconds later it rings and he answers it.

Alec: That's lovely. Thank you. *(he hangs up)* Right, that's us. *(he starts to clear away his tools)*

Trevor: You'll be back on Tuesday?

Alec: Back on Tuesday. Say about half-five?

Trevor: I'll be back up from the shop for that, if I ever make it to the shop again.

Alec: Right then, well sure I'll see you then Mr. Hamilton. Miss Hamilton?

Emma nods. Alec smiles at her.

Trevor: I'll see you out.

Trevor walks Alec out to the door. Emma is smiling to herself and posing into the mirror, checking her hair again and humming quietly to herself. The door closes and Trevor reappears.

Trevor: I thought you were making tea?

Emma: I'm going to, but I thought you had tea?

Trevor: Never have too much tea.

Emma exits to the kitchen. Trevor watches her out, then turns his attention to the telephone and begins practicing answering it again.

Trevor: *(lifts receiver)* Hello. The Hamilton residence. Mr. Hamilton speaking. No, no, no. *(sets receiver down)* Hello. The Hamilton's. *(shakes his head, replaces the receiver and thinks again)* Hello. The Hamilton's five-nine-seven-one. *(shakes his head)* Hello. Londonderry five-nine-seven-one. *(he is happy with this and practices again)* Hello, Londonderry five-nine-seven-one.

During the last attempt, Emma has come to the kitchen door and is watching her father.

Emma: Daddy, what are you doing?

Trevor: *(startled)* What? Oh, nothing. Just getting the weight of it.

Emma: *(setting the tea tray on the table and sitting down facing her father)* Here. Set that down and get that tea into you.

Trevor sits as Emma pours him the tea. He is watching the phone.

Emma: A watched pot never boils, daddy.

Trevor: Meaning?

Emma: Meaning, if you don't stop watching that telephone, it's never going to ring. And why would it ring? Nobody knows we have it and they wouldn't have the number yet anyway.

Trevor: You never know. Maybe we should telephone a few people, just to let them know.

Emma: How many people's telephone numbers do you know?

Trevor looks slightly deflated as Emma falls silent - he goes back to starring at the telephone.

Emma: He seemed very nice.

Trevor: Hmm?

Emma: Yer man. *(Trevor looks at her quizzically)* The telephone man.

Trevor: *(absently)* Oh.

Emma: What was his name?

Trevor: I don't know. I don't think I got it.

Emma: I'm surprised at that. He seemed very polite.

Trevor: *(realising)* Oh! Polite? He wasn't that way before you turned up. I thought I was in an episode of 'The Lone Ranger'. It was 'chief' this and 'chief' that. Aw, it all changed when you came through the door.

Emma: Really?

Trevor: Here, don't you be getting any ideas. He's a soldier. He's in the UDR.

Emma: And what does that mean?

Trevor: I know what them boys are like. He wasn't all full of manners before you arrived.

Emma: Daddy!

Trevor: What?

Emma: That's a terrible thing to say. I thought he was lovely, but I'm sure he'll land here on Tuesday, take the five minutes he needs to do his job and away he'll be off into the sunset. On Silver.

Trevor: Well, we'll see.

Emma moves to the mirror over the fireplace and starts experimenting with her hair. Trevor watches her for a moment and then his attention is drawn back to the telephone.

Emma: Daddy, I think I might go and get my hair done tomorrow.

Trevor: *(rolling his eyes)* Right.

Emma: Just to get a wee bit of shape back into it. It is the enrolment on Sunday.

Trevor: Are you sure it's the GB that is warranting this effort?

Emma: *(aghast)* And what's that supposed to mean?

Trevor: Meaning, is the new look for the benefit of the GB service on Sunday or the benefit of the telephone service on Tuesday?

Emma: *(annoyed, she moves briskly to clear away the tea things)* I think I'll take a wee walk up the town and see if I can get an appointment anywhere.

Emma moves out into the kitchen and when she returns she is moving at speed. She lifts her coat from the back of the chair, not breaking stride as she exits through the hall door.

Emma: I'll see you later, daddy.

Trevor: *(who has been startled by the speed of this movement, stands)* Right, sure I'll see ye....

The door slams and he is left facing out into the hall. He is disconcerted as he notices the piles of clothes draped across the back of the sofa. He moves towards them as the lights fade to black.

SFX of radio news.

Voice Over: *Police in Londonderry last night returned fire from Rosemount barracks, which came under attack at around 2am. There were no reported injuries, but damage was caused to several vehicles parked adjacent to the barracks. In another incident, over thirty families in the Belmont area of the city were evacuated last night when police discovered a device wired to the underside of a vehicle in the area. It is believed that the vehicle belonged to a serving policeman and the families were only allowed to return to their homes when army bomb explosive experts were able to defuse the device in an operation which took over five hours. And now for the weather. Scattered showers will continue throught the night, but these will have passed by dawn and a more settled start to the day should develop into brighter spells in the afternoon.*

Lights up to reveal Trevor setting the table. The clothes have been parcelled up in brown paper and are sitting stacked neatly on the sofa. He exits into the kitchen and enters carrying the teapot, which he sets on the hearth. He then exits to the kitchen again. Emma enters and is slightly taken aback when she sees the table set. Trevor enters with two plates which he is holding on to with a tea-towel. He sets them down and turns to her. There are sausages, potatoes and peas on the plates.

Trevor: *(nervously)* Hello, love. Right on time. Here, give me that coat and sit yourself down there.

Emma: *(unsure)* Thanks daddy.

Emma sits as Trevor pours the tea, replacing the teapot on the hearth, he joins her at the table. The conversation is awkward and interspersed with long silences

Trevor: Did you get an appointment? For your hair?

Emma: Aye. Two o'clock tomorrow.

Trevor: Good. *(pause)* And what time did you get back into work?

Emma: Half one.

Trevor: That's good, you didn't lose the whole day.

Emma: No. *(pause)* No.

They both eat in silence, there is still a residual air of tension between them. They both speak their next line simultaneously.

Emma: Daddy, I thought you were a wee bit hard on the.......

Trevor: It was nice to see you....

Emma: Sorry, daddy

Trevor: No. After you.

Emma: No, daddy, you first.

Trevor: I was just going to say that it was nice to see you smiling today. It's been a while.

Emma: I haven't had much to smile about.

Trevor: No. Well, I just wanted to say it was nice to see. I..... I hope you like your dinner.

Emma: Oh aye, it's lovely. Better than I could have done.

Trevor: Not at all. You'll make somebody a fine wife one of these days.

Emma: *(pause)* As long as it's not the telephone man.

Trevor bristles at this as Emma settles herself as the silence descends on them again as they continue eating. The telephone rings. Both Emma and Trevor are startled by it. They both look at each other for a moment, unsure of what to do. Trevor rises and moves to the telephone looking at Emma. He lifts the telephone and listens.

Trevor: There's nobody there. Oh, hello. Yes. Hello. *(deflated)* Oh. It's for you. Sorry, who is this? *(pause)* Who? *(pause)* Alec Lyttle? Never heard of ye. And you want to speak to my daughter? *(pause)* Who are ye? *(pause)* Aw, the boy that installed the telephone. How did you get this number? *(pause, Emma is delighted)* Of course, you're the boy that installed it. *(pause)* Aye, she is here, aye. *(pause)* Aye. Well, I suppose. But don't be too long, I don't want you blocking up this line. *(pause)* I don't care if nobody else has the number. *(pause)* Right. Well, I suppose so. But like I said not too long. *(to Emma)* It's for you. The telephone man. He's called Alec. *(he hands the telephone to Emma)* *(aside while Emma composes herself)* Smart Alec, if you ask me.

Emma scowls at her father as she takes the phone.

Emma: Hello? *(pause)* *(to Trevor)* He says nobody is asking you. *(they both take a moment to realise he has heard Trevor's remark at the other end of the line)* What? *(pause as Trevor sits indignantly in his chair by the fire, opening up the newspaper and huffing behind it)* Oh, he said nothing. He's just huffing behind the newspaper. *(Trevor folds the newspaper, rises and starts to clear the tea dishes away, exiting to the kitchen)* *(pause)* Really? I don't know. I would have to ask my daddy.

(pause) No. No, I'd love to, but I need to ask. *(pause)* Will I ask him now? *(pause)* He's in a bad mood. *(pause)* Not all the time. *(pause)* Right, right. *(Trevor entering)* I'll ask him now. *(Emma sets down the telephone and moves towards the table, which Trevor is still clearing away)* Daddy?

Trevor: *(ominously)* Yes?

Emma: Daddy? That's Alec on the telephone.

Trevor: Yes.

Emma: And he was wondering if... if he could take me to the pictures on Tuesday night?

Trevor: What?

Emma: The pictures. On Tuesday night?

Trevor: I heard what you said. I just don't believe it. He waltzes in here today, practically demands tea, does half the job and then imagines he's going to start courting my daughter.

Emma: Daddy, please. He was so nice. And he must think I'm nice or he wouldn't be asking

Trevor: Aw, I don't know about this Emma.

Emma: Please, daddy?

Trevor: The pictures? I don't know. I mean, I don't know this boy at all. And those soldiers have a bit of a reputation.

Emma: Daddy, I'm sure he's not like that. *(pause)* Please?

Trevor: *(reluctantly)* I'll tell you what. He's coming here to fix the telephone on Tuesday. If he wants, he can stay for his tea. We'll get to know him a wee bit better and I'll see. Alright?

Emma: Alright.

Trevor: *(lifting the last of the dishes to the kitchen as Emma picks up the telephone again)* Trips to the pictures.

Emma: Look Alec, he says if you want to come for your tea on Tues...... (pause) Oh, you heard. *(Trevor has come back in and is standing in the doorway)* Of course you heard. Well....? *(she signals to her father that he has heard) (overenthusiastic then catching herself)* Oh, that's great. I mean it'll be a nice evening for us all. *(pause)* That's great. Thank you. I'll see you on Tuesday. *(pause)* Goodbye.

Emma puts down the telephone receiver and turns smiling.

Trevor: There's that smile again.

Emma: Daddy, why couldn't I go to the pictures?

Trevor: It's a bit early for that.

Emma: But all the girls from the factory go to the pictures with their...... friends.

Trevor: This boy's getting promoted quickly. Five minutes ago we didn't even know his name, now he's your..... friend.

Emma: What is wrong with him? Why do you seem not to like him?

Trevor: Emma, if I didn't like him, he'd be in and out of here faster than a rat up a drainpipe on Tuesday. Not getting asked to stay for his tea.

Emma: Well, what is it? There's something.

Trevor: It's nothing.

Emma: No, now come on. Tell me.

Trevor: Look, it's nothing. *(pause as she continues to look at him expectantly)* It was just this morning when he arrived. He was.... It was just that he was very off-hand about things.

Emma: What things?

Trevor: It was just something he said.

Emma: *(slightly concerned)* What did he say?

Trevor: Uck! It was nothing.

Emma: Well, if it had been nothing, it wouldn't be bothering you. Tell me. Please?

Trevor: It was just a comment about how there weren't very many Protestants around here anymore.

Emma: And what's wrong with saying that? Sure, it's true.

Trevor: Aye, but.....

Emma: .   But, what?

Trevor: All these people moving out. They're getting better houses elsewhere. That's what it's all about. People just looking for a wee change.

Emma: What? Daddy, that's a lot of people, all of a sudden who are just looking for a 'wee change'. Sure just even look at this street. There were the Wards, the Thompsons, the Roberts, the Nelsons, the Bryants and the Mowbrays. All gone. And that's only this street. You read the piece in the paper about the Protestants having to get out of Bishop Street in the middle of the night, not two days ago.

Trevor: What?

Emma: I know you read it because it was lying open on your knee when I came down this morning and found you asleep in that chair.

Trevor: Aye, but that's all that stuff going on up the town, it's not like that down here. Look, there's still the Hughes, the Deveneys and the Youngs. And us.

Emma: Four families left. Out of street that used to be half full of Protestants. You can't argue with that, daddy. Why won't you realise what is going on? We are being forced out.

Trevor: We are not being forced out. How can you say that? *(moving to the window and pulling the curtain aside)* Look, there's no mob in the street looking to break down our door.

Emma: Do you not feel it? Are you living with your head in the sand? Of course there's no mob. But there's more than one way to skin a cat.

Trevor: What do you mean by that?

By way of answer Emma moves to the sofa where she has left her handbag and removes the mass card from it. She gives it to Trevor.

Emma: Here.

Trevor takes it and examines it, looking at her occasionally in puzzlement. As he is doing so Emma continues.

Emma: It's been going on a long time, daddy.

Trevor looks up at Emma.

Trevor: What's this?

Emma: It's a mass card.

Trevor: Well, I can see that. But it obviously means something more to you than it does to me.

Emma: It was put through the door the other night when I came back from the GB.

Trevor: But, I mean, there's no writing on it. I don't understand.

Emma: You don't understand? Somebody puts a mass card through our door to sympathise with us about our loss.

Trevor: What loss? I still don't.... Maybe it was for your mother.

Emma: If it was for mammy, then somebody would have signed their name.

Trevor: Maybe they put it through the wrong door. Some wane was sent down by his ma to put it through somebody else's door and the wane made a mistake.

Emma: That doesn't explain why it still wasn't signed. And anyway, there's been nobody died in this street recently, so they would need to have got the wrong street entirely.

Trevor: *(incredulous)* So you think it was for us?

Emma: *(long pause)* Daddy, we weren't the only ones to get one. The Deveneys got one last night as well. Mr. Deveney says it's the last straw. *(pause)* They've started packing up. Iris told me. I met her at the corner on my way back up from work.

Trevor: *(heading for the door)* I'm going up to see
            Jack Devenny.

Emma: Don't daddy, please don't. Iris was told not to say.

Trevor: But the Deveneys are part of our church. I can't let
            this just happen.

Emma: Nobody is to know, they're going to go tonight.
            Well, Mr. Devenny isn't. He's going to stay in the
            house at night until they get it sold.

Trevor: Where are they going to go?

Emma: Well, it's not for a nice new house in the Waterside
            anyway. Mr. Devenny has a sister in Limavady. But
            they're not going to be able to do anything about a
            new house until they can get this one sold.

Trevor gets up out of his chair and strides to the mantelpiece.

Emma: Daddy, would we not need to think about moving too?

Trevor: Move? Where to?

Emma: They're building new houses out in Newbuildings.

Trevor: Newbuildings? Do they even have a bus that goes
            out there?

Emma: We could go out there?

Trevor: *(moving to the record player he pulls out the
            loose pieces of paper that Emma stuffed there
            the night before)* So that's what this is all about?

Emma: *(mortified)* Daddy, we're talking about being able
            to live in peace.

Trevor: Peace? Sure we live in peace here.

Emma:　Naw, daddy, we live quietly here. Can you not see what's going on outside that door *(pointing to the mass card)* And now it's come through the door and it's in this house. Most of the Protestants have gone. We're going to have to move too.

Trevor:　I am not going to be intimidated from this house. We have nothing here to worry about.

Emma:　Daddy, are you blind? Not only are we Protestants but my brother, your son, is a serving RUC officer.

Trevor:　And what's that got to do with it?

Emma:　We're going to see David tomorrow, daddy. All nice and safe over in the Waterside, but what if we were followed? Have you told anybody about going to see David tomorrow?

Trevor:　*(considering, but unsure)* I don't know. I don't think so.

Emma:　Are you sure?

Trevor:　Who would....?

Emma:　Who would put a mass card through the door?

Trevor:　How do I know?

Emma:　*(moving to Trevor)* Then how do you know what might happen if somebody heard that we were going to the Waterside to see David tomorrow? What would happen if somebody decided to come through that door one night and lift you out of your bed and hold you and want to swap you for David?

Trevor:　*(incredulous)* Nobody would try to do that.

Emma:　*(taking the mass card out of his hand and holding up in front of him)* How do you know?

Trevor has no answer, he takes the mass card from Emma and stares down at it. He breaks the stare with Emma first and sits down in his armchair at the fire.

Trevor: Is that what's happening? Is that what's happened to our wee town? It can't be. I won't let it be. Should I be the last Protestant on the city side, then so be it. City side Protestants back under siege?

Emma: But this time, no army standing against us. Well, none that will let you see them.

Trevor: *(pause)* Maybe we're doing this to ourselves. The first one moves and the ship is holed below the waterline and now we're jumping over the side, scrambling to get away before the whole thing sinks and we go down with it. *(he looks down at the Mass card in his hand)* Maybe we're not. But where's the help? Where's the loyalty? I stood in the desert defending this country, so that people could be free. So did your grandfather. *(pointing to the pictures on the back wall)* Look, his name's on the wall. No conscripts here. All volunteers! *(to Emma)* Are you the only one who sees this?

Emma: No, daddy, I'm not. But nobody is hearing those that do speak out. *(pause)* Or wants to.

Trevor: What will happen to the church if people up and move away? We'll lose our congregation. The church will close. Maybe I have been blind to all this or maybe the thranness in me won't let me see it. What have we done? What have I done that has caused this? I go to my work, I rear my family, I go to my church. I live as a good neighbour. There was

> never trouble at this door. I just live my life and let others do the same.

Emma: *(handing him the papers with the information about Newbuildings on it)* Daddy, will you think of moving?

Trevor: *(taking them and looking down at them, then resolutely)* No! *(then more quietly)* No.

Emma moves a step towards her father. Trevor turns away from her. Emma, deflated, turns and moves away from him. Trevor moves to the record player and puts on the LP of hymns, playing "I Need Thee Every Hour".

Trevor: *(after a considerable pause)* There are letters from your brother in that left hand drawer in the dresser. They're inside his Derry City hat. The one on the bottom of the pile has a number for the police station he's staying in. Telephone him and tell him not to come down tomorrow. Tell him I'll speak to him at the start of the week.

Emma moves to the dresser and finds the letters. She lifts the telephone and moves out into the hall. As the hymn fades up the lights fade to black out as Trevor pulls the curtains closed.

End of Act 1

Act 2

Lights up. The telephone is ringing. After several rings Emma bursts through the door carrying a bundle of clothes and various other objects, such as board games including Cluedo and Scrabble, a Union flag wrapped round a pole and a few plastic bags. She throws this all down on the floor and reaches for the telephone.

Emma: *(excitedly)* Hello? *(pause, then slightly deflated)* Oh, it's you, David. *(pause)* Sorry, I didn't mean it like that. *(pause)* Well, I wasn't expecting it to be somebody else, but I thought it might have been. It doesn't matter. How are you, anyway? *(pause)* Aye, it would have been nice to see you on Saturday too. *(pause)* I think he must have said to somebody that you were going to be down and then he panicked. *(pause)* I just don't think he realised how serious things are getting. I don't think he wants to. There's something going on up that town every day. *(pause)* I'm sure you were looking forward to getting down. It must be very lonely up there in that barracks all the time. *(pause, then nervously)* I think we should move. I think we need to get out of here, but he won't have any of it.

Emma is about to continue when she hears the front door open.

Emma: Look, there he is. Do you want to speak to him? *(pause)* *(Trevor enters)* Here he is. I'll put him on. *(to Trevor)* Here, it's David. I'll go and get the spuds on.

Trevor: *(taking the telephone)* *(shouting)* Hello son.

Emma: Daddy, you don't have to shout all the way to Armagh, you know.

Trevor: *(realising)* *(to Emma)* Sorry. *(to David)* Sorry, son. *(pause)* Aye, things are grand. I'm sorry I had to put you off there on Saturday, but we're spending so much time out of the shop because of bomb-scares on the Strand that we're just getting so far behind with the orders that I had to work on Saturday. How are you keeping anyway? *(pause as he listens grimly)* Aye, I heard that on the news. *(pause)* Same station as you. *(pause)* He had two wee girls. That's terrible son. Absolutely awful. You make sure and take care of yourself down there. *(pause)* Aw, sure what do we have to worry about? *(pause)* Naw, naw. Things are fine. Just the usual. But it never gets the length of here. *(pause, then grimly)* Have you been talking to your sister? *(turning away from the kitchen)* Look son, she's been inconsolable since your mother died. *(Emma enters, unseen by Trevor)* Sometimes you think she's picking up and then the next minute she's down again. I just think she's very sensitive to everything at the minute. *(Trevor turns and sees the pile of clothes and other objects for the first time and then notices Emma)* Look maybe we'll take a wee run up to Belfast some Saturday and we see you up there, instead of you always trekking all the way down here. *(looking at Emma quizzically)* We'll do that. I'll give you a ring later on in the week. *(pause)* What's that? *(pause)* You're on 8 to 4 for the rest of the week, well sure I'll ring you some evening around tea-time, alright? Here, I better let you get on. I'll speak to you later son. Cheerio.

Trevor puts down the telephone and turns to Emma.

Trevor: Have you been speaking to your brother?

Emma says nothing.

Trevor: *(indicting the collection on the floor)*
             And what's all this?

Emma: I thought it might be an idea to empty out mammy's wardrobe. There's no use all that stuff just lying up there collecting dust. It might give you a wee bit more space.

Trevor:	What are you going to do with it?
Emma:	I was going to give the clothes to one of the charity shops and then, stuff like the games, I was going to save for the sale at the church.
Trevor:	When's the sale?
Emma:	It's ages away yet, but I can get it into bags and leave it under the stage in the hall in the meantime.
Trevor:	*(reaching down to lift the broom handle with the Union flag attached to it)* Where was this?
Emma:	In the back of mammy's wardrobe.

As Trevor starts to unfurl the flag, Emma rises and moves to the window, looking out, she then casually closes the curtains.

Trevor:	I spent the whole week leading up to the 12th last year looking for that. *(noticing what Emma has done, he stops)* Your mother swore blind she didn't know where it was. I was everywhere, even up behind the water tank in the attic.
Emma:	You fell. I thought the house was coming down round our ears.
Trevor:	Well, I'm glad you found it. I was thinking I was going to have to buy a new one this year.
Emma:	*(taking the flag back off him and starting to roll it up again)* It's a bit tattered, daddy. Maybe you should think about getting a new one.
Trevor:	I don't think I want a new one. I like this one, even if it has been a bit beaten up and weathered over time *(taking it back from her)* I'll keep it up in my wardrobe. Then I'll know where it is when I'm looking for it.

Trevor moves to set it in the corner by the press, Emma watches him, but before he turns back towards her, she has got to her knees and started sorting through the various items on the floor, briskly folding all the clothes in four and stacking them on top of each other. Occasionally she looks at an item and decides that it is no good and bundles it on another, separate pile. Trevor moves over to beside her and lifts the game of Cluedo. He goes to sit in the chair by the fire, but doesn't quite reach.

Emma: Daddy, you wouldn't go out and stick a fork in them spuds to see how they're coming on?

Trevor alters his walk to go into the kitchen. Emma continues with her sorting on the floor.

Trevor: *(re-entering)* Still as hard as rock.

Emma: *(moving to rise)* I'll go and turn the heat up.

Trevor: Done.

Emma: What's that?

Trevor: Cluedo. Who committed the crime? Where did they do it? And how was it done?

Emma: It's been a long time since I saw that out.

Trevor: *(sitting down)* Aye. I always enjoyed a game of Cluedo.

Emma: Do ye fancy a game?

Trevor: It was always pointless with two. It always means it's one or other of you. There's no mystery when there's only two. I wonder do we have all the pieces.

Trevor opens the box and instead of the game, to his surprise, he sees photographs, which he lifts out and starts to look at.

Trevor: Well, I'll be....

Emma looks up.

Emma: What is it?

Trevor: Photographs. Nothing else only photographs. Oh, and Reverend Green. *(turning a photograph)* And a photograph of Revered Moore, with me and your mother the day we got married. I bet there's been some great theological discussions going on in this box for the last umpteen years. Not a great fan of the High Church, was the Reverend Moore.

Emma: Oh. What are they doing in there?

Trevor: I have absolutely no idea. *(continuing to leaf through the photographs)* I'd forgotten about these. Look. There's one of your mother and me and David. That was Brooke Park. You wouldn't have been born. David must only have been about three or four in that photograph.

Emma: *(taking up one that has fallen on the floor, unnoticed by Trevor)* Is that Granny Donnell?

Trevor: It is. You would know to look at your granny that she took no nonsense.

Emma: Well, you were courting her daughter.

Trevor: It felt at times like I was courting her. Every time I called, she sat planted in the room and me and your mother trying to whisper to each other, under the clack of her knitting needles. *(indicating the space where his chair is)* She sat here, on a wee stool close to the fire and me and your mother sat there. *(indicating the place where the sofa is)* I would get brought in first and then she would parade in with your mother. We'd sit then for about half an hour and then the tea would be offered and your mother would go out to the kitchen until the tea was made. And sure, didn't that give your granny enough time to get all her questions asked. It always started out the same way. She'd finish whatever row she was on and then she'd stifle a wee yawn and say; "I'll just set this down for a wee minute and rest my eyes." And then the questions started. How was my mother and father? How was work going? What I had thought of the minister's sermon on Sunday? Ye see, she never could see me in the church, because I sat at the top of the gallery and your mammy and her crowd always sat on the floor. And if she wasn't sure I was there from my answers on the sermon, it was always "...and what was that lovely hymn that closed the service in the evening?" And because I worked in Tillies before I went on to work for Mr. Campbell, if she heard any gossip about ones from Tillies being out, she would always recount the story and somehow manage to get me connected in to it, just to see if I had been part of the "rowdy company" that had been too noisy coming out of the pictures, or had been seen going into one of the bars.

Emma: *(sardonically)* Nothing like a watchful eye being kept on ye, sure there's not?

Trevor: *(suddenly slightly awkward)* Looking back on it now, she was right, but she was a frightening wee woman. I wonder if there's any more photographs in that Scrabble box. Pass it over.

Emma passes over the box to her father from the pile on the floor.

Trevor: *(as he opens it)* Feels heavy. *(looking inside)* Oh.

Emma: What is it?

Trevor: The rest of the Cluedo stuff as well as the Scrabble stuff too. Here, why don't you get those photographs out and get the Cluedo back into its box. I'll go and check on the spuds.

Trevor gets up and sets the bundle of photographs on his chair and then exits into the kitchen. Emma separates the two games and puts them into their respective boxes and sets one on top of the other beside her father's chair. She lifts the bundle of photographs and starts bunching them neatly. When she has done this, she starts flicking through the bundle. After looking at several with varying degrees of interest, she stops, looking at the one on the top of the pile in her hand. She stills and looks at it intently.

Trevor: *(entering from the kitchen)* Those spuds are still a wee bit firm, I would give them another ten minutes. What else is to go on with....... *(he sees Emma stilled, not hearing him)* Your mother?

Emma: *(pause)* No, daddy. You and me. I must only have been about two because I'm holding onto your trouser leg and we're both looking at the camera. We're standing out there, just at the door. Somebody must have told you something funny because you have such a big smile. I'm smiling too, but by the look of it, I'm just happy to have you to hold on to. (pause) It must have been near the 12th because there's flags on the front of houses behind us.

Trevor: *(coming over and taking the picture from her, smiling as he remembers)* D'ye see just after that was taken, you fell down. And you hit your knee on the step and cut it. The tears you cried over that. I lifted you up and carried you inside and set you on the sofa and then your mother landed with the TCP and the cotton wool. And that led to more tears. I think they only invented TCP to let you know how much sorer it could have been! This street used to ring to the collective chorus of "Naw, mammy, not the TCP!" every Saturday afternoon. *(enjoying the memory, before looking down at the photograph again and continuing)* I knelt down in front of you and it must have been so close to the 12th that all I could think to do was tell you the story of the Siege to try and distract you. When your bother realised you were getting a story he was straight in beside you to hear about Colonel Mitchelburn and Governor Walker and the Apprentice Boys and Henry Campsie and Lundy and King James. About how the bold King James had come to 'derry to seize it and launch an attack on England and take the throne and how the brave thirteen had closed the gates to keep him out and how the Protestants of 'derry had stood firm against him. I think you were just listening to my voice, for you couldn't have understood, but you never took your eyes off me and by the time I'd finished, you'd forgotten about your sore knee and you skipped back out that door into the street. Of course, I was caught then with your brother and every Saturday night for over a year I had to retell that story at bed time. Bath, Catechism and then bed for the story. Oh, the battles I created, because of course your brother then wanted to be in the story and be a defender too. I think the first time I told that story it lasted about ten minutes, but by the time I was relieved of my post, it was running to nearly an hour. Your brother kept changing it and insisted that the way it finished was that he and King Billy were sword fighting with King James and Lundy at Shipquay Gate because they had managed to sneak aboard The Mountjoy when she broke the boom. If they ever ask your brother to give his account of the Siege it would certainly be a very interesting account to hear. *(pause as he hands her back the photograph)* But where would we be today without those brave people who made, what must have appeared to be, a hopeless stand against those who would have overrun them? *(pause, then emotionlessly to Emma)* That's why I'm not moving. *(more convincingly)* I'm not moving.

Emma: Daddy.....

Trevor: I know what you're doing here, Emma. *(pause)* You're getting your mammy moved out first because there's nothing she can say against it. And then it'll really start.

Emma: Daddy.

Trevor: I'll go and check on these spuds.

Emma gathers up the bundles of clothes and moves towards the door to the hallway. She notices the Union flag in the corner and stops, looking at it, unsure of whether to lift it also. She decides not to and exits as the lights fade to black.

SFX of radio broadcast.

Voice Over: In other news, the local economy in Londonderry
*received a boost today when it was announced
that the American-owned Du Pont were in line to
create another fifty jobs at their Maydown plant
on the outskirts of the city. A spokesman for the
company, which has had its European base in the
city for almost fifteen years, said that they were
"delighted to be able to expand their operations
at the plant and demonstrate the company's on-
going commitment to the north west." In sport
Derry City and Coleraine played out a one-all draw
at The Brandywell last night, despite heavy rain
which had put the game in doubt earlier in the
day. And now for the weather. The heavy rain that
has been present consistently over the weekend is
set to continue until lunchtime tomorrow, with the
afternoon set to be dull with occasional showers.*

*Laughing is heard as the radio broadcast fades down. Lights up to
reveal Trevor, Alec and Emma sitting round the table, Alec on the
stage left chair, Emma on the centre stage chair and Trevor on the
stage right chair. The other, empty chair, is between Emma and Alec.
All three are dressed smartly, Trevor in his waistcoat and suit trousers,
Emma in a good frock and Alec in a pair of trousers, with a shirt and
tie. His jacket is hung over the back of his chair. The tea dishes have
been pushed to the corner of the table and the game of Cluedo is
spread out. The three of them are mid-game.*

Alec: *(to Trevor)* Sure I showed you Colonel Mustard already.

Trevor: When?

Alec: About two moves ago when you accused him of

battering Missus White with the lead-piping in the dining room. *(to Emma)* Your da really has it on for Colonel Mustard.

Trevor: And now you've told Emma, so now she knows.

Alec: She knew before you when she accused him of hanging Reverend Green in the library. Colonel Mustard should just retire from the scene and go back to the front, because everybody knows it wasn't him.

Trevor: I must have forgot to tick him off.

Emma: Daddy, for heaven's sake.

Trevor: What?

Emma: Keep up! How will you know what's going on if you don't pay attention?

Trevor: Oh, right. Whose go is it?

Emma: Alec's. Right, come on.

Alec throws the die and moves six spaces into the Ball Room.

Alec: *(checking his card)* Right, right. I accuse Missus Peacock in the ball room with the.... revolver. Yes. Missus Peacock. Ball room. Revolver.

Emma: Well, I can help you out there.

Emma takes a card from her pile and shows it to Alec, who scores off a name on his card. Trevor tries to watch. Alec notices him and cups his hand round his card.

Emma: Right. My go.

She shakes the die and moves four, but doesn't make it to a room. Trevor then picks up the die and rolls it. He finishes one square away from being in a room. Alec picks up the die and rolls it and moves from the Ball Room to the Conservatory, (which has a secret passage in the corner). He goes to move through that room straight across the secret passage.

Trevor: Here! Where do you think you're going?

Alec: Through the secret passage.

Trevor: Aw, naw. Hold on. You can't do that. It takes one entire move to do that. It's not just like moving one square on the board.

Alec: Aye, it is.

Trevor: Naw, it isn't.

Emma: Rules!

Trevor: Where are they?

Emma: Probably in the box.

Trevor reaches down to the box which is just beside his chair on the floor and reaches the rule book out. Alec, meanwhile, is moving towards the teapot on the hearth.

Alec: Tea?

Trevor: *(under his breath)* Make yourself at home, why don't ye.

Emma: *(aside)* Daddy!

Trevor: *(rising)* Here, that tea's probably stewed. Read you the rules and I'll go and put on a fresh pot.

He hands the rule book to Alec and takes the teapot from him and exits to the kitchen. Alec moves to the empty chair, centre stage, beside Emma and sits down in it.

Alec: Here, you can help me find where it says about the secret passage.

They both lean in to read the rule book, their heads almost touching. Emma is earnestly trying to read the rule book, while Alec is more interested in watching her.

Alec: Are you having a nice time?

Emma: Yes. Yes, I am. Thank you for coming round. It's nice to have a bit of company. It helps to....

Alec: *(cutting her off)* Aye, it's nice to have a home cooked meal.

Emma: I'm not a very good cook.

Alec: I wouldn't say that. It beats fish and chips every night, I'll tell you that. You say you're a bad cook, but at least you can get food to the table. I don't even have a table.

Emma: Why not?

Alec: No need. Fish and chips out of the paper, on a tray on your knee.

Emma: Have you ever had fish and chips out of Fiorentini's?

Alec: I don't know. Where's that?

Emma: Down the Strand. Daddy always brings home the fish suppers on a Saturday. He's been doing that for as long as I can remember. When him and David used to land back from the Brandywell on a Saturday evening, they would have the four fish suppers with them.

Alec: Derry City?

Emma: Aye.

Alec: I'm a Linfield man. I try and see them if I'm back in Belfast for the weekend.

Emma: *(becoming reflective)* Daddy doesn't go down now.

Alec: *(changing the subject)* What did you say that fish shop was called?

Emma: Fiorentini's.

Alec: Fiorentini's? I haven't been there. There's a couple of places in the Waterside I go to. Not that I wouldn't go there, but I usually get something on the way home after work.

Emma: Their fish is beautiful. Really crispy batter. They get that by turning the heat up really high.

Alec: Maybe you could take me there sometime? *(pause)* Perhaps we could go the pictures next week and go in there for something to eat afterwards?

Emma: Aw, I don't know. My daddy.

Alec: Sure, has he not seen what a great fella I am here this evening. Even willing to put the tea on.

Emma: I don't know if he appreciated that.

Trevor: *(from off)* Have you found that rule yet?

Emma and Alec look back at the rule book again.

Alec: Naw, not yet?

Trevor: *(from off)* Are ye's reading that book or..... *(he appears quickly at the kitchen door, both faces look up at him innocently)* Hurry up 'til we get on with this game. *(he disappears back out into the kitchen again)*

Alec and Emma laugh.

Trevor: *(from off)* What's so funny?

Emma: Nothing.

Alec: *(covering)* Just talking about your determination to see Colonel Mustard hanged.

Trevor: *(from off)* There'll be more than him hanged if there's any devilment.

Alec and Emma both laugh again. Trevor comes in with the teapot and a plate of biscuits which he sets on the table. As he enters, Alec rises from the chair he was in beside Emma and moves about, flicking through the pages of the rule book, before sitting back in his original seat, as Trevor places the teapot on the hearth and then sits.

Trevor: I'll let that tea draw for a wee minute. Well, did you find out?

Alec: *(closing the book)* Naw. But sure we'll play by your rules. By the time you've accused Colonel Mustard a few more times, I'm bound to have this game wrapped up.

Trevor "humphs" and rises to get the teapot.

Emma: What about me? I might win.

Alec: I don't mind if you win.

Trevor: *(pouring the tea)* Right, who's go?

Alec: Well, I'm going to have to stay in this room I'm in and accuse somebody.

Trevor: Suspect.

Alec: Eh?

Trevor: Suspect somebody. You're going to have to stay in this room and suspect somebody, is what you mean.

Emma and Alec both stare blankly at him.

Trevor: If you accuse somebody you have to pull out the cards, because you know who did it. At the minute, you can only suspect somebody.

Alec: Oh, right. Sorry. Right then, I suspect Missus Peacock in the conservatory with the revolver.

Trevor and Emma both look through their cards.

Trevor: *(to Emma)* Well, go on then.

Emma: Why don't you?

Trevor: *(pause)* Because I can't.

Emma: Neither can I.

Trevor: Right then, so are you going to accuse?

Alec: Not yet. Play on.

Emma takes the die and rolls it, but still does not manage to get into the room.

Emma: Big 'one'! Great!

Trevor lifts the die and rolls it. He moves into the Billiard Room.

Trevor: Right, I suspect Missus Peacock in the Billiard Room with the revolver.

Emma shows him her card of the Billiard Room.

Trevor: For Heaven's sake.

Alec: Do I need to roll, or can I just move through?

Trevor: Roll the dice. Keep to the rules.

Alec rolls the die and makes a big show of moving his piece from the kitchen through the secret passage and across the board into the Lounge.

Alec: I suspect Missus Peacock in the lounge with the revolver.

He looks to both Trevor and Emma who check their cards and shake their heads.

Alec: Alright then. I accuse Missus Peacock in the lounge with the revolver.

Trevor: Aw, I suppose we may find out.

Alec lifts the small black envelope from the centre of the board and lifts out the cards one at a time throwing them down.

Alec: Peacock. Lounge. Revolver.

Emma: Well done!

Trevor: Aye, very good.

Alec: And now for a celebratory cup of tea.

Trevor lifts the dishes from the table and exits into the kitchen.

Alec: *(calling after him)* Do you want another game?

Trevor: *(from off)* Did you not come here to do a job?

Alec: Oh, aye. I forgot all about that.

Trevor: *(re-entering)* I'll bet.

Alec: I've the stuff out in the van. I didn't want to be bringing it in and have a dirty, old tool bag sitting there all through tea. I'll just nip out and get it.

Alec exits, turning back in the doorway to signify that Emma should speak to her father.

Emma: Well?

Trevor: Well what?

Emma: Well, what do you think?

Trevor: Of what?

Emma: Daddy, he'll be in, in a minute.

Trevor: Oh, him? I suppose he's alright.

Emma: Alright?

Trevor: Well, he seems a decent enough young fella. A wee bit cheeky, mind. But he seems reasonable enough.

Emma: He asked me again... *(pause as she looks hopefully at Trevor)* ...if I would go with him to the pictures and then maybe go and get a fish supper in Fiorentini's. He's never been.

Trevor: Never been to Fiorentini's?

Emma: He's still new to the town. Even just a matinee?

Trevor: I suppose....

With that Alec bursts quickly back through the door. Trevor and Emma are both startled. He is wet.

Alec: It's absolutely lashing out there.

Trevor: So I see.

Alec: I suppose I better get on with this job. I'll grab my tea after.

He sets the tool bag on the floor and opens it up, removing the small-headed hammer, which he sets on the floor and starts searching round the tool bag again getting more frantic as he does so.

Emma: Are you alright?

Alec: I don't believe it. The wee grippers. Aw, don't tell me I've come out without them again!

Trevor: *(aside)* A likely story. Just an excuse to come back again next week.

Emma looks at Trevor by way of telling him to be quiet.

Trevor: *(to Alec)* Maybe you left them out in the van, like you thought you did the last time.

Alec: *(remembering)* I did! I did! I threw a packet of them on the dashboard this morning so they were there in front of me all day. So I wouldn't forget.

Trevor: What? Forget to come up?

Alec: *(smiling as he exits)* Naw. So I wouldn't forget that I had the job to do whenever I got here.

Emma: *(after he has gone)* A matinee? Then I can take him to Fiorentini's after.

Trevor: No. *(pause, as Emma looks deflated)* Let him take you to Fiorentini's.

Emma is excited and Trevor is happy to see it.

Two gunshots go off in quick succession.

Trevor and Emma turn quickly to look out the hall door. They are frozen to the spot momentarily then Emma runs for the hall door, exiting.

Emma: Alec. Alec!

Trevor makes to grab her and misses.

Trevor: Emma! Come back in here. Emma!

He moves out to the hall, but returns again immediately. He reaches for the telephone and dials '999'.

Trevor: Hello. Police. Police and ambulance, please. There's been a shooting. *(pause for a moment as the call is put through)* Hello. Is that police? Hello. There's been a shooting.....

Emma has entered back through the hall door into the living room. Trevor lowers the receiver from his ear and watches, shocked, to see that Emma has blood on her hands.

Emma: *(deadpan, building to a wail)* He's dead. They shot him. He's dead, daddy. His face is all blood, daddy. He's dead.

Trevor drops the telephone and runs out of the hall door. Emma examines her hands and then falls to her knees on the floor, sobbing, as the lights fade to black out.

SFX of Radio.

Voice Over: *A part-time member of the UDR was shot and killed last night in Londonderry. Private Alexander Lyttle was stationed at Caw Barracks in the city. Private Lyttle was off-duty at the time of the shooting and was visiting friends in the Rosemount area. Police sources have stated that they suspect that Private Lyttle had been under surveillance and that a lone gunman had approached Private Lyttle's vehicle as he was preparing to leave the area and fired at him twice, at point-blank range, hitting him in the head and chest. The Provisional IRA, who claimed responsibility for the shooting, said that Private Lyttle, who also worked as a telephone engineer*

*was working undercover for British Intelligence, a claim that
has been refuted by army sources. Private Lyttle, who was
originally from Belfast, had been based in the city for four
months. He will be buried at Roselawn cemetery on Friday.*
(SFX starts to fade) *The Letterkenny Road between Nixons
Corner and the border remains closed this morning after a
vehicle had been abandoned there late yesterday evening......*

*Lights up to reveal the empty living room. After several moments the
door opens and Trevor and Emma enter. They are dressed in black and
have their coats on. Trevor switches on the main light and moves over
to turn the standard lamp on. Emma has entered and is standing in the
centre of the room. Trevor removes his overcoat and jacket and puts
them over the back of the dining room chair on the stage right side.*

Trevor: A cup of tea, love?

Emma does not seem to have heard him.

Trevor: Emma? *(he moves to her)* Emma, love?

He touches her arm, which brings her back.

Emma: Hmm?

Trevor: *(helping her off with her coat)* I said, 'do you
             want a cup of tea?'

Emma: *(absently)* No.

Trevor: Are you sure? Come on now, you must be parched
             after that bus run.

Emma: *(pause)* Alright, then. No. If you're having one.

Trevor: I am. Now, sit yourself down and I'll go and get the
             kettle on.

Trevor half-guides Emma to the sofa and gets her to sit. She sits, still staring vacantly into space. Trevor watches her for a moment and then exits to the kitchen. We hear him moving about. He then re-enters.

Trevor: Do you want a wee slice of toast? *(pause, no response from Emma)* Or a wee biscuit? *(still no response)* Maybe just a biscuit. *(he exits again)*

Emma: We've no bread.

Trevor: *(re-entering quickly)* What was that?

Emma: We've no bread.

Trevor: Oh. Right. *(pause)* A biscuit it is.

He tries to think of something to say, but can't. He exits back out into the kitchen. After several moments, Emma looks across at the dining table. After a few more moments, she rises from the sofa and goes and sits in the chair that she had been occupying when they were playing the game in the previous scene. She sits down in it and fixedly looks at the place where Alec had been sitting previously – staring at it as if she were watching him. After several more moments, Trevor re-enters carrying the tea tray. His pace slows when he sees Emma has moved from the sofa to the table. He sets the tea tray down on the table. Emma's gaze does not waver. Trevor pours the tea for them both and sets a cup in front of Emma. He places the teapot on the hearth and turns back towards the table, moving to lift the plate of biscuits from the tea tray and set them on the table also. After a long pause, in which Trevor drinks his tea and Emma does not touch hers.

Emma: He was sitting just there.

Trevor: Emma...

Emma: So he was, daddy. *(pause)* And then over there, just through that door he was lying dead. It's hard to believe that somebody can be so full of life and then they walk ten steps and it's all over for them. Dead.

Trevor: Emma, love, this is no good.

Emma: Naw, daddy you're right. It is no good. It's all bad.

Trevor: Emma, you're upset, now, please.....

Emma: I seem to have been upset for quite some time. We sat and watched mammy die. I never thought that there would ever be anything as cruel as the way that disease ate her away. She faded away in front of our eyes, bit by bit and day by day. Until she finally just melted out of sight. To have to sit and watch that and know there was nothing could be done and that all you could do was sit and watch. She carried me and was with me every day of my life. *(pause)* As for Alec, I barely knew the man, but his face is never going to leave my head. Sitting in that chair. Or lying with his head on the wet ground and the blood running out of him. It's one thing to have to watch a life fade away, quite another to see one ripped out of somebody. *(pause)* And the boy that shot him, the boy that spilled his blood, the boy that still had his life-blood pumping through his veins to give him the strength to run away. I wonder what image of Alec he has in his head? His look of shock as he turned to see a gun spitting into his face? A gout of blood coming out of his chest? Or him sliding down the side of the van? I didn't see any of that, but I see it all. *(pause)* What does he see?

Trevor: Emma, you have to stop this.

Emma: I can't stop it. It's all I see. You saw it too, daddy.

Trevor: I did. But you have to try and not think about it.

Emma: How? How are you supposed to do that?

Trevor has no answer. He moves past her and heads for the record player.

Emma: *(getting in between him and the record player)*
               No, daddy. No hymns tonight. I've had enough
               hymns for today.

Trevor moves away from the record player, towards the fireplace, where he stands for a moment and then lifts the photograph of him and Emma. Emma moves to him, taking the photograph from him.

Emma: Look at that photograph, daddy and now look at us.
               (Emma makes him look up and they both stare into the mirror) That photograph was taken just over twenty years ago, but it might as well have been a thousand, because the world in that photograph doesn't exist anymore. The people in that photograph don't exist anymore.

Pause as Emma watches her father in the mirror.

Emma: Look at us. *(stronger)* Look at us! *(pause)* We've been changed.

Trevor: No we haven't. We're still the same.

Emma: No we're not! *(starting to break down)* How could we be? After what's been done? How can you say that after what you've seen? We have been changed!

Emma breaks away from him and sits down on the sofa, weeping quietly. Trevor does not know how to react and stands dumb-struck. He turns and looks at himself in the mirror, then down at the clock on the mantelpiece. He sits in the armchair and looks at the photograph. After several seconds the telephone rings. Trevor reacts and rises automatically, moving towards the telephone, lifting the receiver.

| Trevor: | Hello? *(pause)* Hello, Mister Campbell *(pause)* No, we're just back in from that funeral in Belfast today. *(pause)* No, I hadn't heard the news. *(long pause)* Tonight again? *(pause)* No, I understand. *(pause)* Of course. Yes, of course. I'll take a run down there now. *(pause)* I'll be there in ten minutes *(pause)* Right-o. |

Trevor hangs up the telephone. Emma has turned, open-mouthed, to him as the telephone call has drawn to a conclusion.

Emma:	You're not...?
Trevor:	*(starting to reach for his jacket and overcoat, he doesn't look at her)* Emma, that was Mr. Campbell. He got a telephone call from the police to say that some of the shops have been broken in to from North Edward Street and they're asking for key-holders to go and check their premises.
Emma:	*(suddenly panicked)* Daddy, please don't go. Daddy, please?
Trevor:	I have to. I'm sure I'll just be straight down and up again. Don't be worrying.
Emma:	Please don't go. Please?
Trevor:	Emma, I have to.
Emma:	*(moving to him)* Daddy, I don't want you to go.
Trevor:	*(getting angry)* I have to. Now come on. *(seeking to pacify her as he heads for the door)* I'll be up soon. Go on up to your bed.

Trevor exits and the front door slams.

| Emma: | *(highly agitated)* Don't go! |

Emma starts to cry, but forces herself to settle down. Wiping away the last of the tears she takes the stage right seat at the dining table, watching out the open door to the hall. She is still, watching and listening intently. She lifts the tea tray which is propped against the side of the table and sets the used cups and plate of biscuits back on to it. She lifts the tray and rises exiting out into the kitchen. There is sound from the front door. Emma enters quickly, still holding the tray, and pauses just inside the kitchen door watching intently for a moment and then crossing quickly, setting the tray down on the table as she passes and exiting out through the hall door. There are a few moments silence, then a wail of grief and Emma enters sobbing uncontrollably. She has a torn envelope and a card in her hand. She falls to her knees. After several seconds Trevor appears in the door way. He pauses briefly and moves quickly to kneel by Emma, who initially reacts by trying to pull away.

Trevor: *(reassuring)* It's me. It's me. I'm back, I'm back. I'm not going down.

Trevor breaks the hug and holds her at arm's length so she can see it him. By way of response, Emma holds up the card to him. Trevor takes it from her, quizzically, and looks at it.

Trevor: *(reading, in disbelief)* Bang. Bang.

He is shocked and takes some moments to recover, before he starts to get Emma to her feet and lead her towards the sofa. She is still sobbing.

Trevor: Come on now, love. Sit you down there.

Emma: Don't leave me.

Trevor: I won't love. I promise, I won't.

Emma: *(Trevor rises)* Where are you going?

Trevor: I'm just taking my coat off. I'm not going anywhere.

Trevor moves to the press behind the table, opens the door and puts the card inside. *He takes out his tailor's scissors without letting Emma see. He moves back towards Emma, turning off the main light as he does so, leaving only the standard light on and lifting his overcoat as he does so. He sits down on the sofa beside her, setting the scissors on the floor on the upstage side of the sofa, placing a cushion in his lap, she rests her head on it as he covers her with the overcoat. The telephone starts to ring, Emma reacts, Trevor quietens her, not making to move towards it. He strokes her hair as the telephone rings out after six rings. Emma falls asleep, whilst Trevor sits awake and alert.*

Lights fade to black.

Sound Effect of a ticking clock which then fades out

Lights up slowly to reveal Emma lying alone on the sofa, she is covered by a blue blanket. After several moments she stirs awake, slowly.

Emma: *(still half asleep)* Daddy? What time is it?

When there is no response she sits up quickly to see if he is there. When it is evident he is not in the living room, she gets up quickly and moves to the kitchen calling "Daddy?" Then she moves out to the hall, re-entering in an agitated state. After several moments she moves to the chair by the fireplace, looking at the radio for a few moments, her hand reaches for the on-switch as the hall door opens and Trevor is standing there. He is wearing his raincoat which is wet. Emma and Trevor regard each other for a moment, then Trevor enters the room and takes off his coat which he hangs over the back of the stage left chair.

Emma: *(angrily)* You couldn't stop yourself, could you? You had to go down to that shop and do your duty, didn't you? You couldn't leave it.

Trevor: Emma....

Emma: You said last night that you weren't going to leave me.

Trevor: I know, love. I'm sorry.

Emma: Sorry? What's the point in saying 'sorry' because you'd do it again if that telephone rings. What time did you leave here?

Trevor: Just after half-five. The sun was coming up. You were sound asleep. I didn't want to wake you.

Emma: So you left me here, in this house on my own, from half-five.

Trevor: Emma, you've spent every night of your life in this house.

Emma: Things have changed. Or do you not remember why we were in Belfast yesterday?

Trevor: *(pause)* I had to go.

Emma: No, you didn't.

Trevor: It was the only time that I could.

Emma: *(baffled)* In the middle of the night....?

Trevor: I went to the cemetery.

Emma: *(stunned)* Has something...? I don't understand.

Trevor: *(with difficulty)* I had to see your mother before.......

Emma: You were at the cemetery?

Trevor nods, moving to open the curtains to let the morning light in.

Emma: *(pause)* Why?

Trevor: *(turning round and looking at Emma, holding her gaze for a long moment)* The undertaker told me we'd have to go and see them. It took me a minute to catch on as to what he meant. I was burying my wife. I didn't really believe that that was what I had to do until I was actually sitting in the place. Waiting. It felt like I was in the doctor's. I had plenty of experience of that with your mother. Just like the doctor's, waiting for the news to come down from on-high. Final, with no appeal. *(pause)* He came in and sat down in front of me. The undertaker was there as well, but he'd been there before. *(pause)* 'An hour', he said. A little hour. The barrier on the Foyle Road would be open for that long. An hour for us to get in, get your mother buried and get out again. I just sat and looked at him. It felt like I should say 'thank you'. That's how unbelievable it was! *(pause)* The undertaker stood up. He must have, but I never even noticed it, I just felt his hand under my elbow, pulling me up from the barstool. *(long pause)* I didn't think about it again. And then? Then I was standing at the graveside, without time for reflection, barely even prayer. You could feel it from everybody, even the minister. It was like everybody was on their marks waiting for the starting...... I wonder was there somebody somewhere who was timing us. I wonder what would have happened if we hadn't made it out in time. Probably somebody somewhere who was watching us. Watching for David. I wonder what would have happened if he had been there. Not at his mother's graveside? *(pause)* No. *(pause)* The rain was falling hard. It whipped so hard into my face. Covered the tears that I shed in grief, the tears that were rolling down my cheeks. But the rain covered other tears. Tears of shame and hurt at the indecent speed that I dispatched and departed the woman I held and loved for all my adult life. (*to Emma)* You are right. They run this town and they go with their faces covered. Who are they under there? *(pause)*

They regard each other for a few seconds. The telephone starts to ring. It does so six times before ringing off. Neither of them move.

Emma: Me and mammy hid the flag. We didn't want you to put it out. We were scared of what might happen if you did. We didn't want anything to happen to the house.

Trevor: There used to be a lot of flags out in this street.

Emma: There would only have been one last year, if you had found ours.

Trevor: Maybe. *(pause)* Maybe not. Perhaps all it takes is for one person to stand up and the rest would follow.

Emma: It's a big risk.

The telephone starts to ring again. Trevor makes as if to move towards it. Emma moves quickly towards it also, as if to stop him lifting it.

Emma: Don't.

Trevor doesn't break stride. Emma stops as he passes the telephone and moves to the corner where the flag has been standing. He lifts it, examines it and then sets it on the table. The telephone rings out.

Trevor: Clarendon Street is still closed off half-way down and Great James Street is closed off at the sorting office. *(long pause)* Time to go.

Emma: *(confused momentarily)* Daddy, if Clarendon Street is still closed off, you'll not get down to the shop anyway. You didn't go down last night, so why.....

Trevor: We'll go.

Emma: Daddy, I don't want to go down there. I don't want to see anybody or do anything. I just want to sit in this house and pretend that the whole world has gone away.

Trevor: We'll go.

Emma: Go?

Trevor: Away from here. Away from all this. You and me.

Emma: *(confused)* But you said you wouldn't go. You said you wouldn't leave this house.

Trevor: The house? A house is only worth something if it's a home. This place has stopped being a home. This city has stopped being a home.

Emma: What do you mean?

Trevor: A home is a place where people look after each other. Share their worries and their fears. The good times and the bad. That obviously stopped happening here long before your mother died. I just didn't see it. *(pause)* I didn't know how worried you were whenever I went out. I can't have my own son visit his family 'home'. Or the same thing will happen to him as happened to that young man we laid to rest yesterday.

Emma: Did you see his daddy?

Trevor turns away.

Trevor: Fathers shouldn't bury sons. The oldest of four brothers and the other three weren't even big enough to take a lift on the coffin. Oh, I saw it. It wasn't lost on me.

Emma stands and watches her father for a moment until he composes himself and turns back to her.

Trevor: Well?

Emma: Well, what?

Trevor: Are you not going to take some stuff with you?

Emma: But what about all the furniture? We have a house full of our things.

Trevor: We'll have to leave them.

Emma: Leave them? But, it's....

Trevor: Emma, go and pack a bag.

Emma: This all seems very sudden.

Trevor: It has all happened very quickly.

Emma: But what about you?

Trevor moves to lift a suitcase, where it has been sitting behind the dining table and sets it on the table.

Emma: When did you do that?

Trevor: Before I went to see your mammy.

Emma: You knew?

Trevor: *(pause)* I remember you being born in this house. In this very room. It was a Sunday morning and whenever David and me came back from church, the nurse had arrived and was with your mammy. *(nodding to the corner of the mantelpiece)* Your granny was in her spot to supervise everything. Your mammy was well on by the time we got home, she went into labour just after I had left to take David up to Sunday School. She told me after that she wanted to have you before we got back, because she didn't want to see David upset with her in pain. So as soon as we got back, your granda was standing at the door waiting and we went for a walk, on up Park Avenue and out at the top of Creggan Hill. We walked down and over Marlborough Street and then down onto the Lone Moor Road and then back up along Foyle Road and Foyle Street, along the Strand and back up Clarendon Street and Academy Road. Back up to the house. And poor David – the wee man was exhausted and starving, but all that fell away whenever he came into the house and your mammy was back up in her bed. I knew you were born as soon as I came through the door, because your granny was smiling and believe me, that didn't happen very often. I grabbed David up in my arms and ran up the stairs and there you were lying in beside your mammy, wide awake and those big brown eyes of yours taking everything in. David was all full of questions and I couldn't answer them for smiling and laughing. Memories like that are too precious to let other ones, bad ones crowd in over the top of them. Your mother is gone. There's nothing that could be done about that. We don't see David, because we've become estranged from him because of these troubles. And you and I are going to tear each other apart if we don't change it. I don't want that. *(Emma nods) (pause)* Go. And pack the things you'll need.

Emma exits the sitting room. Trevor watches her go and then moves to the blue blanket that has fallen to the floor. He moves behind the sofa to look out the window, pulling the net curtains aside to look out. When he drops the curtain he looks down at the record player. He pauses for a moment, then opens the lid. He finds the pieces of paper that Emma had previously relating to Newbuildings. He lifts them and looks at them briefly before putting them in his inside jacket pocket. He turns the record player on and moves the needle across onto the record. "The Day Thou Gavest Lord" starts to play. He listens to it for a moment. After the first two lines he folds the blue blanket and places it over the back of the sofa. He moves to the table where he has set his bag. He looks at the pictures on the wall, the Honourable Discharge, the photograph of David in his RUC uniform and the picture of himself in North Africa. He looks at them for a moment and then takes them down from the wall, putting them into a plastic bag that he takes from the press.

The day Thou gavest, Lord, is ended,
The darkness falls at Thy behest;
To Thee our morning hymns ascended,
Thy praise shall sanctify our rest.

We thank Thee that Thy church, unsleeping,
While earth rolls onward into light,
Through all the world her watch is keeping,
And rests not now by day or night.

As o'er each continent and island
The dawn leads on another day,
The voice of prayer is never silent,
Nor dies the strain of praise away.

Trevor moves downstage centre surveying the room, a look of melancholy about him. Emma enters and stands in the hall doorway. She has put on her coat and is carrying a bag.

The sun that bids us rest is waking
Our brethren 'neath the western sky,
And hour by hour fresh lips are making
Thy wondrous doings heard on high.

As the fourth verse is drawing to an end, Trevor turns and notices her in the doorway.

Trevor: Time to go.

So be it, Lord; Thy throne shall never,
Like earth's proud empires, pass away:
Thy kingdom stands, and grows forever,
Till all Thy creatures own Thy sway.

Emma nods. Trevor makes his way to her lifting his two bags and the rolled up Union flag. They pause to look back into the room one last time and exit, closing the door behind them as the music builds to the end of the hymn and the lights fade, lighting the spot on the wall where the photographs were, which then fades to black out as the sound effect of a stylus rotating at the end of the record continues in the dark for a moment.

Silence.

The End.

The Exodus Transcripts

Throughout the research process for "The Exodus", countless interviews were undertaken as part of the project, which fed into the creation of the script. In the following pages are verbatim excerpts from those interviews. The overwhelming majority of the people who gave those interviews expressed the wish to remain anonymous due to fear of being identified, even today. Therefore none of the sources are named.

There is no continuous narrative or sequential order to these pieces. Each one is an individual statement (whether a few words or sentences) concerning an individual moment, a personal reflection by someone on an aspect of their personal exodus. These small insights come together to reflect the mood and the enforced change undergone by individuals, in microcosm, which represent the reality of that time and the legacy of hurt for that entire community.

The following are the transcripts on which the Exodus Play was based. These are the recorded details directly from those affected by the troubles at the time.

Before The Exodus

I was born and reared in the Glen, the house we lived in, in Glenside Park, I was actually born in.

....

I grew up with mixed company, up behind me was Harley's, Roddy's, Stewarts, all that there, the Quinn's. It was all mixed company, that I run about with at the top, with a lock of my mates, and then, we were about, starting secondary school, we started secondary school then, it was Templemore and it wasn't what you would call mixed, it was all more or less Protestants at the school. There was no bother then.

....

I'm from Academy Road originally – a prefab house. Big family. My father was a bricklayer. We lived happily with our Catholic neighbours.

....

One night, most of the friends I had were like myself, in the boys choir in the Cathedral and the girls were in the girls choir, so we were all sitting one night and the girls had learned this "All In The April Evening". So some started to sing, so we started to harmonise with them, you know, all the boys out of the choir. There was Brian Turner and Derek Morris and me and my twin and everybody else. And the next thing ye saw was Maud Hunter and Jan Edgar and all this and they all came out and we sort of looked at each other but kept on singing and I remember the place was as quiet, it really was quiet and when we were finished they all started to clap.

....

We couldn't believe this, that they were all.... and the Woodcocks came out of their shop to come up round the corner and listen and all this here and we had to sing it three times and I remember thinking, 'music is the charms to calm the savage breath'. But that was the Fountain. That was our fun.

....

After the war, we lived in Bishop Street which was mostly commercial. My great-grandfather was a sweetie-maker in the early 1900's. McIlroy was his name. It was a very cosmopolitan area. Protestants and Catholics.

....

Born on the 10th of September 1959 at the City and County Hospital, just up onto the Northland Road, Londonderry My mother died in childbirth and I was brought out of the hospital, I think it was three days after I was born, by my father and my aunt. My father was in the Royal Navy, obviously home for the birth but tragedy as well. I was brought home to the Foyle Road - 53 Foyle Road.

....

Then, the sort of thing was, we started running with our own company, our own kind, sort of thing, we always still spoke to our mates, at the top end of the estate, but sort of running with our own kind, sort of thing, and then more or less, when the bother really set in, we sort of, run then with the boys at the bottom end of the estate, it was mainly all Protestant at the lower end.

....

I remember ye lay in your bed at night and you knew everybody's footsteps coming down the street. You knew who was coming in home and say "There's John Arbuckle", or "There's Trevor McAllion" or whatever coming down the street. That's how close everybody was, how much of a community. And Joan Skeet and Marion Logan and all, you knew their high heels coming down the street or you even recognised peoples door closing, I could tell you who's door closed.

....

I lived on the Foyle Road with my granny and granda who were my mothers parents, my mother then of course having been deceased, so I was brought up by them. My childhood was mostly spent in and around the Foyle Road. In my very early years my Granda, who was a former engine driver in the GNR would have taken me across the road and I would have been up on the footplate of steam engines when I was two, three - pre-school age and probably until I was about four because that was when the GNR shut down. We lived in a basic two up two down house, the parlour was the front room, the good room, no body went into really, the back room or what we called the kitchen was just a back room where the TV was. Black and white TV, table, washing line above in the ceiling and then there was a scullery out the back, wooden scullery, and outside of that was the back yard and beyond that was the coal shed and the toilet, the attic had been converted into two bedrooms, so we didn't have anything really, just the basics like everyone else. Riverview Park was a playground for us where everybody gravitated to. Riverview Park. And ye took your old shoes, because you had three pairs of shoes. You had your old shoes where the toes were kicked out of them and then you had your shoes for school and you had your good shoes for Sunday because not only did I go to First Derry Primary School but I also went to First Derry Presbyterian Church and of course when you got new shoes, the old Sunday shoes became your school shoes and the school shoes became your kick-about shoes and that's what ye had.

The Exodus

There would have been the odd altercation between boys on the estate and factory boys. The army and the police would have lined the front of the estate. Funny enough, the factory boys, never would have ventured into the estate. At night there was maybe ten or twelve boys went into one of the factories for like shift work. At times they would have come through the estate. Other times they wouldn't have, but there would have been nothing said, coming through, but if anything started, we had nowhere to go, so we were always stuck in the green in the middle of the estate, I saw altercations at times there.

There was more intimidation, or fear ye know, peoples hearts were changing like, as well, sort of scary too ye know because you think of like Bosnia, ye know, ethnic cleansing, but this wasn't ethnic cleansing like Bosnia, this was more like a sort of psychology. Intimidation by words and all, ye know, words, through a process of time.

....

People just felt under threat, brutal intimidation.

....

The first bar we went into was Danny Grants in the Fountain, right up into the corner of the Fountain. We went in the Mem. It would have been the main bar, we would have sort of been in the wee snug, but most night's was taxis, to pick us up and take us home, the earlier part of the night, we would have got the bus, and just straight up the street and in. Out of the way.

....

I remember on bloody Sunday and I was standing at the top of the street at the shops and ye automatically came back down the street a bit because the shots were coming from the left hand side. You thought they would be shooting up the street again, so I stood and then somebody said, "The army's shot people in the Bogside" and all this. And then there was more stories coming, so they reinforced the barricades because we knew that that night the Fountain would be attacked again. And whenever we heard what had happened, the whole place was in uproar. Nobody celebrated in the Fountain. Nobody was going, "That's great", or "That's whatever".

....

The IRA campaign originally was between them and the British Army, but as time progressed they began bombing businesses on the west bank. Along the Strand Road, Thompson Edwards Motor Works, Craig's Engineering, Heaton's Bakery, Hill's Department Store, Warwick's paint shop, Cloakie's Glassworks, Northern Ireland Electricity. All the way up the Strand Road was targeted. They then started targeting Protestant civilians, under the guise of attacking business men and it became increasingly obvious that anybody who was a Protestant living on the west bank, it wasn't a good place to bring up your family, so a lot of people left.

....

The biggest problem for anybody living on the west bank of the Foyle and one of the main reasons for the exodus was that anybody with teenagers, especially sons, they could not let those sons out and at night and walk freely around the streets. They couldn't go to the Boys Brigade, they couldn't go to the youth club, they couldn't go to the scouts, they couldn't go anywhere because they would have been assaulted.

I was born in 1964 and lived in Belmont (near Shantallow) on the west bank until 1972 when we moved to Lisnagelvin on the east bank. In Belmont, we lived in a very mixed street. I recollect getting on well with our Catholic neighbours and indeed one of my best friends was Catholic. There were also some police families on the estate and as a child at that time I was not aware of sectarian tensions despite the constant news items regarding the civil rights campaign and then bloody Sunday.

When I was much older, my parents told me that there were rumours in the street that a man with a gun was intimidating Protestants on the estate. One day my mother had been visiting a neighbour at the end of the street and was walking back home when she heard footsteps behind her and noticed a man running up towards her. Bearing this rumour in mind she ran up to the front door and banged on the door to be let in. The man followed her up to the door but then revealed he lived down the road and only wanted to warn her of the risk. For a time after that, my Dad kept a hammer near his bed in case of any trouble! When we moved to Lisnagelvin to a new housing development, many of our old neighbours became our new neighbours. However, this time the demographics were different with 95% of the area Protestant. Up to the age of eight, I had Catholic and Protestant friends. From the age of eight, I had only Protestant friends. As a teenager, the troubles had coloured my attitudes to the "other side". Five people I knew to speak to were murdered by the IRA on different occasions, one of the was a former policeman neighbour of ours in Belmont, shot dead as he left church with his children, who we used to play with in Belmont. Things were now so different to when we could live together in Belmont without mistrust. There was one occasion when we (a group of teenage friends) intimidated a Catholic family nearby by burning a tricolour outside their house. We still went to school, church and Boys Brigade on the west bank, but no longer to visit friends or relatives as they had all moved to the east bank.

....

We came out of there in '77 just after April '77. My father was UDR and he was shot dead outside the house. Aye, that's what brought us over here.

....

The next thing I saw this black thing pass me, about a foot in front of my head. It was a half brick and now if you understand you would have had to of thrown it quite a distance to reach me from where he was, he was probably no more than fourteen himself, but there was a bit of venom there and the only reason why he wanted to throw the brick at me was simply because he knew I was a Protestant.

....

A lot of people, the majority of people were refusing to go, they kept saying, "This is where I was born". It was my home and everything, but very, very nervous. Nobody was happy leaving!

....

People that were married and in their thirties or whatever, they moved to Newbuildings and places like that, and to me Newbuildings was at the other end of the world, I didn't even know where Newbuildings was until I was about sixteen.

....

The older people and the younger people didn't go, and there was quite a few with the 'No Surrender' attitude. Had I had a say in my own thing, I wouldn't have gone. That was my home, that was where I was brought up and the people that did go, most of them regretted it, very definitely regretted it.

....

I was born in Londonderry in 1961 and lived in Shantallow. My school was beside the Bogside and our church was in Great James' Street. My dad was in the RUC, a senior detective. He worked long hours. We never knew if he was coming home. Our phone was a hotline during the troubles. We lived on the banks of the Foyle and the noise from the town, either shooting or bombing, carried up the river. We weren't allowed to tell anyone what our dad was. He was a 'civil servant' but the reality was that everyone knew us. At the start of the troubles we lived alongside out Catholic neighbours. After 'bloody Sunday', I remember getting out of the car after going to church and our Catholic friends starting calling my dad a Nazi. We didn't play with them after that. I wasn't allowed to go to school for a few weeks after bloody Sunday, because there was a threat on police families. I remember going back to school and being frightened walking up the long drive where the houses backing onto our playground had black flags hanging into our playground. In school you had to carry a hanky because of the tear gas. Your eyes would start watering and the teacher would go round shutting the windows quickly. The rioting would start from early afternoon most days. During Operation Motorman, dad was on duty. Mum knew but didn't tell us. She kept me up for company. A knock came to the door. After shouting out "Who's there?" - we had to do this, we didn't open the door until we knew who was there. Some security! It was someone from dad's work. She let him in and screamed and yelled "He's shot, isn't he, he's shot. It's the head, they shot him in the head". As it turned out he'd been in the Creggan estate in the grounds of a school on his own and had fallen down a bank and broken his leg. The caretaker's dog found him and eventually the caretaker came to his rescue. There were some good people after all. As I said before we weren't allowed to open the door. No security glass, no intercoms. You just stayed well back and shouted "Who's there?" Our friends were moving 'across the water'. We moved in 1972. We just didn't feel safe any more, but life was just as bad there. I also remember spending quite a few Sunday afternoons watching RUC funerals with mum. I remember these well, the band played the funeral march and the RUC hat was on top of the coffin. "There'll be no band at your dad's funeral' mum used to say". He's one of the lucky ones who is still alive today. It's painful to talk about.

....

They actually carved "IRA" into the front door. That was something! Just somebody had taken a pen knife or something like that and carved "IRA" into the front door, about two or three inch-tall letters, but never the less. Obviously that's the sort of intimidation, some would say non-violent, because it was not directed at people but it was obviously there as a threat.

....

We had no shops, nothing at all on the estate. We had a mobile van, but they went out at a certain time, so we were all smoking then. From, I suppose, twelve onwards, thirteen up, sort of thing, so if you were looking for cigarettes we had to go to the other Glen, opposite the Milanda Bakery, which would have been out of bounds for us more or less. But, we went there and when we went out for cigarettes, there was about, maybe ten or twelve of us, had to go up, safety in numbers, you sent two boys to the shop and the rest of the boys sort of watched them, to make sure there was no bother. Got a bit older then, you were looking for a drink, the off licence was up there too. Same thing, squad of us went, when you wanted to get something.

....

The houses there, they were all painted red outside, sort of this shiny red that gave them all character and I remember the petrol bombs and the paint bombs and the bricks and bottles and, ye know, everybody started moving, ye know and you didn't know what to do, so we stayed on.

....

Mrs Wallace, run a club and we got all our stuff through her, ye know the DM's and the boot's and the Skinners and stuff like that, ye know, we ordered stuff there, ye know. Me father was a foreman at DuPont and he was in the UDR and stuff, it wasn't big money then, but still, what you got was made to last ye and I was lucky enough, because he would have got me the steel caps, brogues, out of DuPont, so I was one up on everyone else. As we got older then, we were going into the town, we had Crombie's and skinners and the boots and all, we also had a Tartan, it was a Blue Tartan, we called ourselves Apache Tartan, we'd the blue, the other boys in the Waterside had the red and the other boys had white, We'd the Blue, Apache Tartan. But if we were seen in the town, it was just a walloping, if there wasn't enough of us.

....

Wee Jinny Taylor, who couldn't have defended herself. She was unfortunately the first house inside the Fountain from Bishop Street, and her house was attacked mercilessly, and Mrs McPheeters was an old woman who lived opposite her and she was in her 80's and she was petrified. She was petrified and that's how she ended her days in fear of attack and whenever the barricades and all went up, the police asked us not to do it. We had no choice, we had absolutely no choice. It was elderly people at that end of the Fountain, the Fieldings, the Murphys, we just had no choice, they had to be protected. It was inconvenient because instead of going into Bishop Street, you had to go away down to Carlisle Road, and up, to go to church, up past The Diamond, and things, but it was the only way a body could live. The constant roars at night and the fighting and you could hear from Creggan and the Bog and the smell of tear gas and the burning and the smoke, it just wasn't a pleasant existence.

....

As the troubles kicked of in 1969 obviously, this being the cockpit of the troubles, the area that I played in or that I felt safe in, became somewhat confined to just outside the door and then eventually to the house itself. I couldn't stand at my front door.

....

One of my cousins had to go and stay out the Glen with his sister for a while because of the rioting at the top of Lewis Street. He went up to the house then one lunch time, to check the house and the house itself had been set on fire. It was burning when he arrived. Some had been burned out and then it kept spreading. It was a whole mass exodus of the Protestants over there.

....

But the situation on the Foyle Road then became worse, because the young Catholics, started to target me, started to cat-call, started to throw stones when I was walking along the Foyle Road and I then got a bicycle, not so much because I wanted a bicycle, but because I felt it was safer to travel from the Foyle Road to Lincoln Courts by bike than it was to walk. And it wasn't the length of the walk and it wasn't that I was walking through an area that was unknown to me on the Waterside that nobody would have known me. It was the fact that I was walking in my own area I'd lived in then for thirteen, fourteen years and I felt really vulnerable. In addition, a youth club was opened, it was a port-a-cabin affair opened on the old railway track on the Foyle Road, and that attracted a lot more young Catholics and it became a case of running the gauntlet on Foyle Road when I was coming back from the Waterside. Not so much going to the Waterside, when you went early, you went in day light, and I was probably fourteen at this stage, it was when I was coming back. I remember one night in particular, there was an army base on the Foyle Road, just at Craigavon Bridge and the youth club was beyond that and my house was beyond that again, and I had to run the gauntlet. But because the army base was there, the lights on the Foyle Road were out, so I was going through darkness I was passing Riverview Park, the playground of my youth, yet had now become a possible ambush point and as I walked along the Foyle Road, the wall of the park, I always looked up, always look up and be very wary of somebody coming over that wall. And of course when you got to the end of the wall, there was the corner and you had to watch yourself going round the corner as well, I was travelling straight across the Foyle Road but you were then in the area where the youth club was and the houses were and the people were and yeah just very, very wary.

....

I remember it was raining, and we were in the Fountain and there had been a lot of trouble that day. Somebody said that there was a fight at the Memorial Hall - the Memorial Hall was being attacked, so we went down and over London Street because the top of the Fountain was blocked and we went down and Willie King, I remember he was in London Street and there was a lot of other people there. There was maybe ten or twelve people and there was police there and there was noise coming from the Diamond, it wasn't at the Memorial Hall and I remember walking over to the end of the street and the police. The police went down towards The Diamond and there was some people walking up and this time Willie King came walking up, he was looking for his son, Stuarty. He wanted his son, and he walked out and I saw him walking out, but I turned and went back over London Street towards the Fountain and the next thing I was walking and people were running past me shouting and all this, and Willie King was on the ground and there was about six men and they kicked him and kicked him and kicked him, and they killed him, he was lying on the ground dead.

....

Stuarts beside us had gone already. Harts had gone already. The Harts moved to the Fountain, Stuarts moved to the Waterside, and the McCartneys on the other side had actually gone to Belfast. Mrs Graham at the end of our road, she was left, she was there and every other house then ye know when the Protestants moved out the house either remained derelict, it was either squatted into by Roman Catholics or moved into by Roman Catholics. Mrs Graham had been the only Protestant left on that road when we moved. We were one of the last to move in relation to the rest of our relatives who had lived in Rosemount and wherever else, they had already moved. We were the last to move out, I think maybe last or second last, aye I think Burnetts were living in Manse Street in Rosemount, they may have been after us but I'm not sure, I think we probably were the last if not second last.

I remember the troubles. We could smell tear gas all the time and I remember everybody telling us to get a damp cloth and tie it round our faces and the Fountain was attacked on a nightly basis, sometimes three of four times, so they built a barricade at the top of the Fountain, looking into Bishop Street, one in London Street, you know to stop attacks from Bishop Street coming in. I remember the bottles and the petrol bombs coming flying over the walls all the time.

Well, it was August '71 the Dark Lane episode was. It all kicked off with The People's Hall getting burned. It was the time of internment and they were putting barricades up all over the place and they put a barricade between Gordon Place and Windmill Terrace and that barricade meant that the Protestants in Gordon Place couldn't get in to their houses. And John Hart, who had been on holidays in Portrush came back and couldn't get into the house and he was a very high ranking officer in the Orange. So what happened, the contacts were made with the Fountain for to go down and bring his furniture out. How I came to know about it, I was in Corporation Street with my parents and a knock came to the door about 7 o'clock and one of the sons said to me about the father's predicament and could I go and help at 8 o'clock and I said I would. So I went to the top of Corporation Street to see what was happening, so just with that the soldiers came round. They had been in the jail at the time and they didn't even put on their gear. They were in plimsoles. They came rushing down into Barrack Street, the bru was there at the time and I was standing at the bru and these two people approached me and asked me what was going on. (I knew one of them from Alexander Place and I knew he had connections with the paramilitaries.

He knew me because we were brought up together.) I said, "I don't know". He said, "The army is going to complicate matters here". There had been more excitement down the Dark Lane than I was aware of at that time. People had got word that this was going to happen and there was high excitement because the barricade was up. He said to me, "Is there any way you could get rid of the army?" And we could make a passageway into Gordon Place. I said I'd se what could be done, so I approached the army boy that was in charge and said I'd been asked to see if they could withdraw and that the people who put up the barricades would accommodate us. Then the other boyos said that they would give me a guarantee that two priests would come up from the parochial house and stay with the Protestants until the furniture was moved out. I relayed that to the army and whether they confirmed that with the parochial house, I don't know, but two priests did come on the scene and the army withdrew and about 8:30pm the lorry came down from Fountain Street and went into Gordon Place. They started loading up the furniture and by 4 o'clock in the morning, thirteen families had been evacuated. There was no trouble during that time and John Hart's son and myself were the last two to leave Gordon Place and we walked up with the two priests who had stayed in Gordon Place the duration of the night and early morning and we left them and I went home.

....

I was asked if I could drive a lorry and I said "Aye". It was just a matter of going to a house and putting a couple of bits of furniture on and then going to the next house and putting a couple of bits of furniture on. Everything was just getting dumped on and, of course, people were saying, "I want this". "This is sentimental to me". I had to turn round and say there was no sentimentality here. It's a matter of getting out or there'll be big bother. It was heartbreaking to bring people out of the houses, when they had been living there are their lives. The older people were standing crying like youngsters in the street because they were losing everything.

....

The problem with taking the lorry into dead-end streets was getting back out again and the people were standing. Just rev the lorry and keep going.

Thompsons in Shipquay Street was bombed. Aiken's Garage on the Foyle Road was bombed. Andrew's Garage in Abercorn Road was bombed. Jackie Sterling's was bombed and there were other shops up round Bishop Street were burned.

....

Before she died, she said she wanted buried in the City Cemetery and for some time prior to that Protestants didn't get access to the City Cemetery. The barricades were all over the place. So, Jim Daly, the fellow who was burying her said that somebody was going to have to go and see them, so myself and Robert went with him down into the Bogside Inn. We sat down and three boys came in with the masks on, sat down at the table and Jim Daly said about the old lady being dead and we were her relatives and they never looked at us at all they just said they would open the Foyle Road barrier from 2 to 3. We came down the next day and the barrier was open. A wild, wet day. We went across, put the old lady in the ground scarpered again and were away within the hour. Nobody got up to the grave afterwards. It wasn't a time when women went to the grave yard, but the fact was that until the barricades were down, nobody visited that grave at all.

....

A Sunday afternoon, we used to watch the rioting. They used to come up Barrack Street. They used to throw rocks down into Abercorn Road. Anyway, this Sunday, the soldiers were coming up St. Joseph's Terrace and they crossed the street onto our side of Abercorn Road and there was an entry just on the bend. Anyway the first boy goes across, the second boy goes across and the third man. Bang. He went down like a tonne of bricks. I resolved I was getting out at that stage.

....

It was purely and simply because of the fact that you were a Protestant that you did feel under threat.

....

I wouldn't have moved, I didn't want to move, but there was a re-development going on at the same time and we were told that if we moved out of the Fountain, we would get housed in Lincoln Courts but because after six months we could apply to come back to one of the new

houses that were built in the Fountain. So we moved over, but we were told you can't paint the walls for six months until the plaster all dries and settles and settlement cracks were dealt with and all this, so we didn't. We lived with grey walls for six months, in the knowledge that you were going to move back to the Fountain, but when the six months were up, we went down to the housing executive. I have to say me mother never settled in the Waterside, never ever did. So we went back to the housing executive to say that we were told this. They said no, that we would be pointed now on the house that we were living in. We were told we had no chance at all, so we never got back to the Fountain. But prior to this, between the bomb outside Woolworths and then shortly after that, Willie King was kicked to death in London Street and he, he lived just across the garden wall, our two gardens were separated by a wall and my mother took it really badly.
....

Nobody came up the Fountain to apologise for Willie King, Bobby Stott or Billy Logan or ye know any of the people who were murdered that were from the Fountain. Nobody ever came and apologised. Nobody ever wanted an enquiry. Bobby Stott worked in a factory, he was from a poor family and he was my friend. And he came up from his work to his house in the new Fountain, for the first time ever they had central heating in their house, first time ever, and he was shot, in the Fountain and then whatever coward did it, stomped on his face whenever he was lying on the ground.
....

We eventually moved from the Foyle Road in 1975, my Granda had put in for a house in 1969 so either it was foresight on his part or he experienced something that I wasn't aware of in terms of knowing it was time to go, but you don't, it was his family home. The only incentive that I could have thought for him leaving was because of the attacks on me, but it was obviously something that must have happened prior to that, because I remember him saying he had been in six years for a house. We eventually got a house in Nelson Drive with a bathroom, moved on the 4th of July 1975. Independence day and it meant more when I look back on it now in terms of independence than what I thought it was noted for in terms of the American War of Independence, but 'Independence Day' for us was moving away from Foyle Road and I remember Mrs Doherty next door, well I didn't see her, but I was told she was in tears the night before that we were going. So that was a community that was a victim, the community was the victim.

....

It leaves you cold. You become a cold individual, with no love in you. You separate yourself from people, from your family because you might be next and you don't want them to be hurt.

The Legacy of The Exodus

My brother, his wife's mother still lives in the Cityside, not the Fountain. My sister always says I don't know how they stay, but they just keep themselves to themselves, the neighbours know though.

....

The interesting thing is, we moved to Gobnascale, up there, from the city side to Gobnascale, but there was IRA. We were forced out of there too, I remember my mother saying. They were shouting and all at night and scaring people, "Prod's out!" Prod's were in Gobnascale, you see, at the time when they developed the new estate in Holymount. You see that's what it was too ye know, Gobnascale was being built for the exodus, people were moving out of the city side and Prod's were moving in.

....

But the IRA was there you see.

....

A lot of people moved to the Waterside with resentment of what they had to go through and that resentment is still there.

....

The people who still live in the Fountain must feel even more isolated. I stayed there for twelve years until 1989. I had four children and my wife said "You can stay if you want, but I can't bring my children up here". It was like living in a birdcage. They couldn't go anywhere. As they got older and came eleven, twelve, thirteen they couldn't go into the town centre, they couldn't even go outside their own area in broad daylight or they would have been targeted for abuse.

So everything had changed, but we had been branded and we had been, if you like, identified as Protestants, more so moving out of that area, than we had been in my mind when we lived there. Because I had always lived there and loved it.

....

We were in the Glen the other night and I was with this American bloke and I was saying, can you believe that this here was all Protestant at one time and they were all driven out, ye know, through time they left, I don't know how many years it took the Glen to empty.

....

We left and even though I return often because this is where I was brought up, I would never think of bringing a family up here.

....

I remember, now this was the end of the '80's, standing at the top of John Street and having to time your run so you would see the Newbuildings bus coming round the bottom of John Street, so you would arrive at the bus stop just as the bus got there, because you couldn't wait at the Newbuildings bus stop.

....

Its always a minority, a wee group, friction, terrorises the community, you've all them wee young boys running around ye know the streets they're mobs like that put your windows in or throw petrol bomb's ye know, once they get control of an area, they'll terrorise it.

....

I came out then, to the Waterside, whenever my father was shot, we came over here and we had no community houses or nothing then.

....

Nelson Drive, which became a Loyalist area, but it was really, if you want to describe it as an area, it's a refugee area, because a lot of the people form the Glen estate and the West Bank, had come over to Nelson Drive, a lot of them after I had done, but then the Glen Estate was a more solid Protestant community that eventually dissipated into nothing. But they became the new Waterside people if you like. I mean I would never have described myself as a 'Waterside person'. I would now, but not then.

I went to Foyle And Londonderry College and when I moved to Nelson Drive I just got the bus straight across, with my new bus pass, because I lived so far away! We didn't have before that.

....

I do remember every incident more or less. They say most people do, but I think its because of the being aware, being alert, looking out for yourself, making friends, losing friends, experiencing things, that were not nice, that probably carved out a very modest individual, I don't know. People might say I'm not modest, ye know, coming out more since I've joined the Apprentice Boys and reached out to other people and made new friends and things like that, but I still maintain that that modesty that I attribute to Presbyterianism, but I also attribute it to not being able to speak my mind and not being able to say things, because you knew if you did, it would probably get a reaction that wouldn't be nice. You didn't go out and shout your mouth off on Foyle Road about being Protestant.

....

It was grand over here at the start like no bother or nobody really to fight with us.

....

It was that joyousness of being able to go out your front door and not have to look over your shoulder. That was really good.

....

We still went over to church over to the Cathedral, still, she went across to the town every day, but she never settled in the Waterside. She was never happy.

....

There's a bond between the people of the Fountain that can never ever be broken and it'll never be again, with any other community. The community was taken out of the place. I remember the day they knocked down our old house and remember the big lead ball swinging and it hit the wall and I took a brick. I still have it somewhere out the back. This was my grandmother's house that we lived in and there were ten of us lived in it. We had and outside toilet, we had no running hot water, there were two bedrooms and eight children slept in the three double beds in the front bedroom and my father and mother in the back bedroom, sometimes if there was a baby, their cot was in there. In the winter there was a paraffin heater on the landing that was used for about two hours to heat up the rooms, and whenever we all went to bed it was turned off in case we were poisoned. Ye know, we had fantastic parents, we had fantastic neighbours. There were no rich people in the fountain.

....

Freedom! You could stand at your front door.

....

I drove over and they had knocked down all the old houses and rebuilt new houses. I knew where the house was. The whole place has changed, but there's a tree there now. There is no other house there now. I loved that.

....

Well everybody says they were never brought up to hate anybody and that's understandable. Nobody is. But there was hatred developed within that community and in many ways there was probably a bit of a hatred for the people who threw the stones and carved the initials 'IRA' in the door and that, but these were faceless people I hated, they weren't actually people I knew. They weren't actually people I had been friendly with and then all of a sudden had become an enemy. I said about Tony Doherty, I remember coming across Foyle Road in my Foyle uniform and Tony was sitting up on the Riverview wall and he spoke to me, because Tony knew who I was and I knew who he was and that was good. There was no hatred there, yet Tony had gone into the encampment of the Roman Catholic side, if you like and I was part of the Protestant side that they wanted out. I would love to meet him again actually, love to meet him again. I don't know if he's still alive or not.

....

You can't compare it with anything, there was nothing to compare it to.

....

I miss the wee house in the Fountain with the fire and the winter nights. Ye used to fill a shoe up with slack and put it on and us all sit round it. I miss the smell of the gas cooker in the scullery. I miss, well maybe not miss so much, but I miss shouting "Don't be puttin' your cold feet on me", or whatever when we got into bed and we had a single bed that my twin and I used to sleep in and there was a bed that Lynn and Noreen slept in, and a bed Kenneth and Ivan slept in by the time Kathleen, the eldest had got married. Sharon had a cot in the back room with my father and mother. I miss it believe it or not. The winter mornings when ye got up and the frost and the ice was on the inside of the window where you were breathing and it had frozen in the window. I miss standing out in the back yard on a summers night with the dog and hearing Jimmy Logan calling in his pigeons, or Raymond Walker calling in their pigeons or Josie King getting ready to go out on a night out and calling at somebody to turn the something or other on so she could curl her hair. That was my life, that was all I ever knew. I remember the slates falling off the roofs on a stormy day, ye know. I remember Gretta Dalzell and Evelyn Corothers and Lennox Keats and everybody standing there leaning on their brushes in the street in the afternoons and I just remember so much, I remember the poverty, I remember if somebody had got new curtains, it was a whole talking point because this was great for somebody was doing well. People moved to Newbuldings and things like that, but the troubles destroyed the Fountain, the redevelopment did more damage and I don't know what else to say to you.

....

The legacy of the exodus is to have polarised the people in 'derry dramatically. I could take you to people who haven't been over the town in years. The wee town over there has become cut off. It has been left to the Republican ideals.

....

We're probably all damaged, but we're damaged in a way that we know what the word 'respect' means. We know what the word 'hate' means, we know what the word 'good' means, we know what the word 'evil' means, because you can define these things by your experiences. You weren't sheltered from any of it, it was all there.

....

I'm giving you this interview now because this story has to be told. In many ways, probably part of the difficulty we have in expressing ourselves is that we have never been given the opportunity until now, until the likes of these interviews are sort of scripted and retold.